Earth Shadows on the Sky

Earth Shadows on the Sky

The Holy Trinity, Divine Sovereignty, and Humanistic Philosophy

H. A. HOPGOOD

WIPF & STOCK · Eugene, Oregon

EARTH SHADOWS ON THE SKY
The Holy Trinity, Divine Sovereignty, and Humanistic Philosophy

Copyright © 2021 H. A. Hopgood. All rights reserved. Except for brief quotations in critical publications or reviews, no part of this book may be reproduced in any manner without prior written permission from the publisher. Write: Permissions, Wipf and Stock Publishers, 199 W. 8th Ave., Suite 3, Eugene, OR 97401.

Wipf & Stock
An Imprint of Wipf and Stock Publishers
199 W. 8th Ave., Suite 3
Eugene, OR 97401

www.wipfandstock.com

PAPERBACK ISBN: 978-1-7252-7532-4
HARDCOVER ISBN: 978-1-7252-7533-1
EBOOK ISBN: 978-1-7252-7534-8

Scripture quotations are from The Authorized (King James) Version. Rights in the Authorized Version in the United Kingdom are vested in the Crown. Reproduced by permission of the Crown's patentee, Cambridge University Press.

Italics in Scripture quotations are original.

Extracts from The Book of Common Prayer, the rights of which are vested in the Crown, are reproduced by permission of the Crown's patentee, Cambridge University Press.

08/31/21

To Dr. Peter Toon, who first led me to understand the beauty and centrality of the Blessed, Holy, and Undivided Trinity.

Contents

Acknowledgments	ix
Introduction	xi
Chapter 1 | The Basis of Theology	1
Chapter 2 | Definition of the Ontology of God	23
Chapter 3 | Development of the Orthodox Doctrine of God's Ontology	34
Chapter 4 | Post-Reformation Rationalism—The Puritan Position	56
Chapter 5 | Effects of the Enlightenment—Charles Chauncy and the Liberal Position	69
Chapter 6 | Effects of the Enlightenment—John Gill and the Conservative Position	88
Chapter 7 | Becoming Theocentric	99
Glossary	121
Appendix	125
Bibliography	129
General Index	139
Author Index	143

Acknowledgments

I wish to express my indebtedness to James Hayes, ThD; for his help and encouragement. I owe much to Elizabeth Hopgood, MA; for her direction and for discussing and delighting in historical theology and the Holy Trinity with me. I wish to thank Stephanie Hopgood, Doctoral Candidate; for typing the manuscript and providing both theological and editorial insights. I also wish to thank Pastor Stefan Lindblad, Doctoral Candidate; and Pastor Stephan Hicks, MB; for their advice and insights; and Deacon Gary Wilkinson and Deacon Paul Nemeth for reading the manuscript. Special thanks goes to Gloria Gaupp, MA; for critiquing and correcting the grammar. *Soli Deo Gloria.*

Introduction

Earth shadows on the sky are caused by the sun's rays striking a geographical body (such as a mountain) at a low angle, causing its shadow to be projected upward. From man's limited perspective he is continually in danger of projecting his own conceptions and theories upward onto God instead of receiving the image of God through revelation from above.

> It is right for the ordinary Christian—and for the philosopher too, for when he stands at the font or kneels at the altar he is as 'ordinary' as anyone else—to state his faith in the most commonplace and straightforward way that he can; but it is also necessary to remember that because we are enmeshed in the created order—because we are, so to speak, at the thin end of the Creator-creation relation—we habitually see everything upside down.[1]

The outworking of this inverted view of God is most evident in theology regarding God's sovereignty and the freedom of man's will. Misconceptions of God's sovereignty spring from misconceptions of God's nature, or ontology, due to the application of humanistic, anthropocentric reasoning as evidenced in the primacy of the doctrine of soteriology and subordinationism in the doctrine of

---

1. Mascall, *Christ, the Christian, and the Church*, 43.

Introduction

the Trinity in the teachings of Charles Chauncy (1705-1787) and John Gill (1697-1771).

A study of the writings of Charles Chauncy and John Gill is a study in comparison and contrast. Charles Chauncy, a proto-Unitarian Universalist, and John Gill, a committed Trinitarian with hyper-Calvinist leanings, both reveal the influx of rationalism in their interpretation of Scripture. Both men had a spiritual background in the Puritan strain of the Reformed tradition; both were well studied in the current theological and philosophical theories of their day. That both should exhibit to different degrees the same doctrinal weaknesses regarding the nature of God and incorrect, though opposite, views of God's sovereignty demonstrates that those dangers do not lie merely in one's position on predestination or man's free will. The real problem lies in the misconceptions of God's nature that, in turn, arise from a wrong view of the relation of reason to Scripture.

Although leaders of their respective movements, Charles Chauncy and John Gill have received a great amount of bad press during their lifetimes and since.[2] Such *ad hominem* attacks fail to acknowledge that these men were zealous for the right understanding of doctrine and for the good of their fellow men. In failing to recognize this, the critics fail to detect where the two men went astray. The result is that the critics can and do fall into the same errors; therefore, the point is to learn from these two men's mistakes.

As leaders, Charles Chauncy and John Gill did not begin movements as much as crystalize and systematize teachings that had been developing in a broad, undefined manner. Both men were widely read and had superior mental faculties. Furthermore, both desired to preserve and advance the doctrines that they had received. Unfortunately, their writings do not evidence serious attempts to evaluate those received doctrines by Scripture as a whole but merely to support them by individual Scripture texts. Such mental confines are by no means unique to the Puritans. People from all eras have worked to reconcile to the point of absurdity

---

2. See Oliver, "John Gill (1697-1771)," 162. This has proved true of Charles Chauncy also.

Introduction

the differences within the theological and philosophical concepts they have received without stopping to consider whether those concepts accorded with divine revelation or if other orthodox possibilities existed.

Yet Charles Chauncy and John Gill were indeed leaders. The philosophically adapted theology that they consolidated has affected thousands until this present time, especially in America. Most significantly, the definition they gave to their opposing schools of thought makes their writings valuable in identifying the errors to which all Christians are prone.

This book focuses not as much on the questions concerning sovereignty as what questions should or should not be asked and how those questions should be approached. In order to obtain a clearer view of theological concepts and to situate the persons in their proper historical context, terms and positions are defined by the ancient ecumenical councils and creeds, as well as the writings of the Protestant Reformers. Although the general Puritan background of Charles Chauncy and John Gill is briefly described, the doctrinal teachings of these men are chiefly represented by their own writings.

Furthermore this study relies on the excellent work that has already been done regarding the doctrine of the Trinity, especially in its historical development. Hopefully, as this is brought together with the seventeenth- and eighteenth-century writings, some light may be shed on the sovereignty debates. However the study assumes that though the church as a whole increases in knowledge of God, true theology supersedes any single historical setting.

> Thus we may be saved from committing that peculiar sin against history which consists in reading back into the documents or the formulas of an earlier period ideas or conceptions which properly belong to a later one. But if this be the peculiar transgression which violates the true historical method, it is at the same time to be borne in mind that this very fact implies that due weight is to be given to formal or logical considerations, as well as those that are specifically 'historical.' For chronological sequence is not the only kind of sequence; there is

Introduction

a sequence of thought which is independent of time; and of this fact historical students need to sometimes be reminded.³

Herein lies the benefit of historical theology for today.

H. A. Hopgood, ThD, DREd
Reformation Day, 2018

---

3. Bishop, *Development of Trinitarian Doctrine*, 19–20.

Chapter 1

The Basis of Theology

THE COMMON CLAIM ON SCRIPTURE

Scripture is the source of all truth for theology. Because of this fact nearly all theologians have referenced, if not relied on, Scripture for their study, whether they lived before AD 500 or after AD 1500. However, while they assert a common claim that each one's theology is scriptural, various opposing theologies do exist. "It is somewhat disconcerting to realize that Christian theologians who have appealed to the same biblical authority have not infrequently drawn opposite, or nearly opposite, doctrinal conclusions."[1] If it is assumed that Scripture does not contradict itself and cannot be read with contradictory meanings regarding those truths which pertain to God's nature and man's eternal salvation, whence come these mutually exclusive doctrines? The answer lies in how Scripture is employed.

---

1. Gammie, "Journey through Danielic Spaces," 269.

Earth Shadows on the Sky

The Ancient Church

The ancient church writings and councils present one method of using Scripture. Those writers acquired the authority for their arguments from Scripture, even if they illustrated from other sources such as nature or common human experience.[2] These writings *still* resonate with Scripture at nearly every point, *still* are read as timeless, and *still* are studied for their theological worth.

However, the writers of the conciliar period[3] did not merely employ Scripture to support or defend their arguments and conclusions: they began with Scripture, but they also compared and corrected themselves and other theologians by Scripture as they proceeded. A brilliant argument was not universally accepted unless it could be demonstrated to be in accordance with Scripture on all points.[4] Otherwise, if an opinion departed from Scripture, it was classified as heretical. Like scholars today, these writers appealed to former authors whose writings had themselves been compared with Scripture in their day; nor did these writers treat the human authors whom they cited as equal with Scripture in authority. "Great as was the respect paid to the fathers, there was no question of their being regarded as having access to truths other than those already contained explicitly, or implicitly, in Scripture."[5] Nowhere was this commitment to and reverence of scriptural authority more evident than at the conciliar conventions. While the exact details will be addressed more fully later, a few points should be observed beforehand.

Whereas the apologists had used Scripture as a shield against paganism,[6] the church fathers of the conciliar period used Scripture as a shield against heresy.[7] In doing this they first strove to stay with the exact words of Scripture to describe and confess the orthodox

---

2. Kelly, *Early Christian Doctrines*, 46.
3. See glossary for definition.
4. Dionysius of Alexandria, "On the Promises," 146; see also Kelly, *Early Christian Doctrines*, 46.
5. Kelly, *Early Christian Doctrines*, 49.
6. Justin Martyr, "First Apology," 260–76.
7. Athanasius, "On the Incarnation," 36–37.

The Basis of Theology

faith.[8] Only when, at the first ecumenical council of Nicaea, the heretics assigned to each phrase of Scripture a meaning contrary to another part of Scripture were the defenders of orthodoxy ultimately constrained to depart from the actual words of Scripture and introduce new words to encapsulate and safeguard the meaning of Scripture.[9] Such a move led to a great outcry in some congregations, and members of the council had to defend the change.[10]

The use of Scripture as both the foundation and the building stone in the work of the church fathers in confessing the faith is highly evident. Confession of faith, however, was not the only time when the authority of Scripture reigned supreme in their considerations. The didactic writings of this time, which were primarily exegetical, exemplify how these men were willing to oppose the accepted philosophy of their day or to modify that philosophy to bring it into conformity with Scripture as the Scripture required. (The attempts of a churchman to fit the Scripture into the current philosophy shall be discussed in its place.)

Perhaps the greatest display of the early church fathers' use of and respect for Scripture appears at those points of exposition or teaching when they acknowledge their own inability to comprehend the whole meaning of Scripture or to explain the whole nature of the God they worshipped.[11] They did not pretend to have command over the mysteries like some pagan priests, nor did they try to explain away those mysteries or to adjust them to an easier philosophical palatability.[12]

The Enlightenment

Such an approach to Christian mystery has not always characterized the church. During the Enlightenment of the seventeenth and eighteenth centuries, the increasing changes in thought concerning

---

8. Kelly, *Early Christian Doctrines*, 46.
9. Athanasius, "Defense of the Nicene Council," 162–64.
10. Eusebius of Caesarea, "*Epistola Eusebii*," 5.
11. Latourette, *History of Christianity*, 1:163.
12. Dionysius the Areopagite, "Our Knowledge of God," 42–52.

Scripture, philosophy, and doctrine crystalized. New views arose regarding the nature of man's ability to reason. While Scripture had been the test of all thought and opinion in the early church, reason now became the lodestone to which all thought must be brought.[13] The pressing question was no longer "Is it scriptural?" but "Is it reasonable?" This change of focus held profound implications for Christian teaching.

Theologians of the Enlightenment era[14] did not abandon Scripture. Even the most radical theologians like Samuel Clarke usually appealed to Scripture at some time to support their opinions or those of others.[15] Yet then, as today,

> Even where there is a vocal commitment to the inerrancy, inspiration, and authority of Holy Scripture, pantheism and natural religion can be present in the hearts and attitudes. This is because in this case the attitude to the Bible can be at the level of commitment to an ideology rather than as an expression of living, personal faith in the Father, the Son, and the Holy Spirit—the Blessed, Holy, and Undivided Trinity.[16]

For these theologians, all theology, even Scripture itself, had to conform to the standards of human reason.[17]

In order to standardize reason, Enlightenment thinkers relied heavily on creation, that is the natural order, and common experience.[18] This order is the inverse from that exhibited by the writers of the conciliar period. Those writers used Scripture as the basis of their argument and illustrated that argument from the created order and common experience, while the Enlightenment authors used nature and experience as bases and supported or buttressed

---

13. Webb, "Emergence of Rational Dissent," 18–21.
14. See glossary for definition.
15. Clarke, *Discourse Concerning the Being and Attributes of God.*
16. Toon, *Our Triune God,* 20.
17. For a modern example of this approach, see Wiles, *Making of Christian Doctrine,* 12.
18. Webb, "Emergence of Rational Dissent," 19.

The Basis of Theology

their arguments with Scripture.[19] Mankind was to be the origin of any definition, including that of God's nature. By this means the Enlightenment theologians projected their own concepts of deity onto God instead of receiving his revelation of himself from above. The earth was casting a shadow on the sky.

Not all theological writers and thinkers of the Enlightenment era relied equally on reason. Some did rely heavily on Scripture. Even they, however, experienced the extreme pressure, not merely to show that they had used Scripture logically, but that Scripture was logical in and of itself.[20] John Calvin's warnings came to pass as the greater part of the Protestant pastors set foot on shifting sand.[21] They often failed to critique philosophy by Scripture, choosing instead to find what seemed like the most logical philosophy or the one that seemed to explain man's most pressing questions. Furthermore, many of those who sought to interpret Scripture by itself from an orthodox standpoint developed a rather mechanistic approach that minimized or completely removed a need to rely on the Holy Spirit when interpreting Scripture and applied a rather physical/materialistic method of deriving scriptural meaning.[22] Protestant teachers and writers of the Enlightenment era felt the need to prove or to understand all knowledge, despite their acknowledgment that some divine truths were mysteries. Gradually logical proof was not sufficient either; empirical evidence was required.[23]

Since nature and human experience appeared to provide sufficient empirical evidence, few perceived the irrationality of proving spiritual truth from physical perception. Although opposing theories arose at this time regarding the nature of human perception[24] and the reasoning process,[25] which raised numerous controversies to the point of evoking indignation among philosophers, few

19. May, *Enlightenment in America*, 12.
20. May, *Enlightenment in America*, 12.
21. Calvin, *Institutes*, 1.1.7.4–5.
22. Toon, *Hyper-Calvinism*, 16; see also Pelikan, *Bach among the Theologians*, 38–39.
23. Webb, "Emergence of Rational Dissent," 21.
24. Kuklick, *Churchmen and Philosophers*, 16–18.
25. May, *Enlightenment in America*, xiv.

realized the absurdity of relying on that which was itself not fully understood for understanding of the most vital truths.

The liberty and impiety that many assumed on these bases alarmed the more conservative and earnest in the church.[26] They, in turn, sought to defend orthodoxy and Scripture but, alas, from the same ground on which it was attacked.[27] The temporary gains these debates and arguments won only served to slow the influx of rationalism's conclusions into the church, making rationalism itself more easily assimilated. The tremendous intellectual pressures brought to bear upon the Protestant teachers and preachers of the Enlightenment era should in no way be minimized; neither should those same forces be overlooked in the conciliar period any more than in this day and age. Therefore, to understand the correct relation of Scripture and reason is extremely important.

USE OF SCRIPTURE

Understanding Scripture Spiritually

Scripture is a book of spiritual truth. That is to say, the main *raison d'etre* for the writings of Holy Scripture is to reveal Christ, who is "the Truth."[28] Its varied references to history, nature, and social experience are not as much designed to inform people on those subjects as to point to and instruct concerning Christ.[29]

The apostle Paul indicates the need for a spiritual approach to Scripture in the First Epistle to the Corinthians.[30] His is not the only instruction on this point. The apostle Peter in his second epistle, the Epistle of James, as well as the Epistles of John and Jude refer to the necessity of spiritual understanding in dealing with Scripture, especially in contrast with carnal/worldly knowledge.[31]

---

26. Webb, "Emergence of Rational Dissent," 17.
27. Toon, *Hyper-Calvinism*, 42–44.
28. John 14:6; 5:39.
29. Benjamin, *Simply Singular*, 43.
30. 1 Cor 1.
31. Jas 3:15–17; 4:4; 2 Pet 2:12; 3:17; 1 John 2:20–21; 5:20; Jude 10.

The Basis of Theology

Of course this approach was not a novel invention of the New Testament era. The Psalms contain innumerable comparisons and contrasts between natural/carnal perception and spiritual understanding.[32] The prophets also deplored the lack of spiritual understanding in the people of God in their day and the doleful effects of that lack. "My people are destroyed for lack of knowledge: because thou hast rejected knowledge, I will also reject thee, that thou shalt be no priest to me: seeing thou hast forgotten the law of thy God, I will also forget thy children."[33]

Scripture must therefore be understood in a spiritual manner. Such is the nature of the subject under consideration. One must not approach a piece of great literature in the same manner as a geological formation. The result would be a perverse rendering. Moreover, unlike moving from one scholastic discipline to another, a person cannot simply decide to change from carnal, physically based thought to that which is spiritual. Spiritual thought has to be a whole way of thinking about anything.[34] Spiritual thought develops the virtues which, in turn, are indispensable in interpreting Scripture.[35] To distinguish between moral disciplines, such as Benjamin Franklin exercised,[36] and true Christian virtue is important. True virtue loves God with the whole heart and one's neighbor as one's self, which is quite beyond the reach of mere morality. It is, rather, the fruit of the Spirit.[37]

Spiritual understanding comes from the Spirit of God. Like the psalmists and the prophets, the apostles insisted upon the need for God's Spirit to enable men to think spiritually.[38] The apostle Paul teaches that the Spirit of God, as the origin of revealed truth and spiritual life, communicates the truth of God's word to

---

32. Pss 14:2–3; 82:5; 92:6; 94:10; 107:43; 119:27, 99.

33. Hos 4:6; see also Isa 5:13; 44:19; Jer 4:22; Hos 4:1; Mal 2:7–8.

34. Calvin, *Institutes*, 1.1.2.1.

35. Gregory of Nazianzus, *Faith Gives Fullness to Reasoning*, 218. See also 2 Pet 1:3–8.

36. Franklin, "Autobiography," 100–3.

37. Mascall, *Christ, the Christian, and the Church*, 82–83. See also Gal 5:16–26.

38. 1 Cor 2:12.

believers.[39] The Spirit testifies of Christ.[40] The author of a book is its best interpreter; the same is true of Scripture. Yet even beyond the basic level of literary evaluation, the Spirit is able to overcome human weakness and inability because he has the power to open or close minds.[41] "The entrance of thy words giveth light; it giveth understanding unto the simple"[42] but only as God opens his people's understanding and hearts.[43]

> For as they [the Scriptures] came not by the will of man, so may they not be drawn or expounded after the will of man: but as they came by the Holy Ghost, so must they be expounded and understood by the Holy Ghost. . . . Thou must therefore go along by the scripture [sic] as by a line, until thou come at Christ, which is the way's end and resting-place.[44]

While humbling to human nature, this is joyous news. God's people can know what is beyond natural perception by the operation of God's Spirit. "*That which* I see not teach thou me."[45] A believer can proceed confidently (but not overconfidently in the flesh) to understand and interpret Scripture.[46] "For, while the process of revelation attained its completion in the manifestation in human flesh of him who is, simply and finally, Prophet, Priest and King, so that nothing remains to be revealed which was not given in him, the displaying of all that is involved in that revelation is one of the great works of the Holy Spirit in the Mystical Body."[47]

---

39. Rom 8:5.
40. John 15:26.
41. Job 28:21; Isa 29:10; Acts 16:14; 1 Cor 2:10; Eph 1:17–18.
42. Ps 119:130.
43. Luke 24:45.
44. Tyndale, "An Answer unto Sir Thomas More's Dialogue," 138.
45. Job 34:32.
46. Augustine, "On Christian Doctrine, III," 154–58.
47. Mascall, *Christ, the Christian, and the Church*, 241.

The Basis of Theology

Interpreting Scripture by Itself

Not only is such divine illumination necessary for initial entrance into spiritual thought, it continues to be indispensable every time a person considers a biblical text. Spiritual quickening and illumination have at times been confused with enthusiasm.[48] Having the gift of the Spirit will not suffice in interpreting Scripture. However, Scripture itself forms a safeguard against bizarre or heretical interpretations since it provides limitations, guides, and warnings on how it is to be interpreted. The Holy Ghost, in testifying of Christ, who is the Word of God, and speaking not of himself but from Christ, requires believers to use and respect the guiding and guarding aspects of Scripture.[49] No passage of Scripture can be read against another. Numerous theological positions exist and have existed that interpret one passage or concept in Scripture in a manner inconsistent with, or even in flat contradiction to, other passages of Scripture. The most glaring example of this may be Marcion,[50] who interpreted the New Testament to be at complete variance with the Old Testament regarding the character of God.[51]

> No place of scripture may have a private exposition; that is, it may not be expounded after the will of man, or after the will of the flesh, or drawn into worldly purpose contrary unto the open texts, and the general articles of the faith, and the whole course of the scripture, and contrary to the living and practicing of Christ and the apostles and holy prophets.[52]

Scripture must consequently be interpreted by itself; that is, interpretation of any part of Scripture must accord with all and every part of Scripture.[53] This is not to say that every hermeneutic

---

48. Theodore of Mopsuestia, "Commentary on Galatians 4:24," 151–52.
49. John 16:13–15.
50. See glossary for definition.
51. Latourette, *History of Christianity*, 1:125–28.
52. Tyndale, "An Answer unto Sir Thomas More's Dialogue," 138.
53. Calvin, *Institutes*, 1.1.9.1.

must be complete before it is usable, but any interpretation that is found contrary to another part of Scripture must be revised.

Such revision and interpretation with regard to the corpus of Scripture takes a great deal of thought and the application of both wisdom and discernment. Although the necessary wisdom must come from the Holy Spirit, as previously mentioned, God continually admonishes his people throughout Scripture to think, study, and give diligence to those things he has revealed to them.[54] Diligent use of the mind in pursuing biblical interpretation undoubtedly employs reason. The mind (or soul)[55] cannot be passive in contemplation of spiritual things.[56] How that mind is equipped, prepared, or conditioned will make a serious difference in how a person interprets Scripture. Not all wisdom is from above.[57] Therefore philosophy, defined as the love of wisdom, differs based on which wisdom is loved.[58]

Interpretation of Scripture is inferior to Scripture itself, as the study of the original will never equal the original. This may appear self-evident at first, but it is more disturbing upon closer examination. Truth, not doctrine, springs ready-made from the pages of Scripture. Divine revelation is viewed through the human eyes of an interpreter. The limitations and frailties of human nature restrict one's ability to know and understand God, although, as noted above, these restrictions do not prevent him from knowing and understanding God altogether since God has promised through his Spirit to make himself known to his beloved people.[59] The place and result of interpretation is doctrine.

---

54. Mascall, *Christ, the Christian, and the Church*, 241. See also 2 Tim 2:15 and 2 Pet 1:5.

55. Matt 22:37; Mark 12:30; Luke 10:27. The exact relation or identification of the mind and the soul is beyond the scope of this work. Scripture indicates that both mind and soul must think and love God.

56. Augustine, "Divine Providence," 320.

57. Jas 3:15–17.

58. Augustine, "Divine Providence," 271.

59. Num 12:6; Prov 1:23; Ezek 20:5, 9–12.

The Basis of Theology

The Development of Doctrine

The development of doctrine, or more specifically of dogma, occurs as believers contemplate and teach the truth of Scripture.[60] Man, even while taking Scripture as a whole, naturally assembles its various statements concerning any one subject in order to define what is to be believed regarding that subject. Because this is necessitated by the human thought process, almost all regenerate minds do this to a greater or lesser degree to find answers to questions.

This movement from many truths to one truth, which is in turn related by principle to many others, is the objective development which also leads from one literary genre, Scripture, to another literary genre, doctrinal (or creedal) statements. While most Christians are content to receive these statements from others, the statements themselves only come into being as those who are practiced in focusing on truth both in experience and in the abstract (that is, determining the relation of one truth to another truth) compare "spiritual things with spiritual."[61] This is, in turn, the result of a subjective change in which understanding is accomplished in the intellect instead of with the whole person, which is differentiated instead of undifferentiated consciousness.[62]

Differentiated consciousness refers to the pursuit of truth as truth for truth's sake. One must bring all of one's energies, usually expended in feeling and physical activity as well as thought, to bear solely in the service of mental activity, called colloquially "brain work." In undifferentiated consciousness the imagination invents a goal; the feelings or emotions embrace the goal; the mind devises the way to accomplish the goal; and the body completes the actions to achieve the goal, aided by the will which choses that goal above others. In differentiated consciousness the imagination must supply suggestions regarding how to arrive at the truth; the feelings and emotions must be controlled to prevent their interference with the view of the truth; the mind must act upon its knowledge and the

---

60. Mascall, *Christ, the Christian, and the Church*, 230–35.

61. 1 Cor 2:13.

62. For the basis of this discussion of the development of doctrine I employ the explanation of Lonergan, *Way to Nicea*, 1–17.

suggestions of the imagination in order to discover the truth; the body must support the needs of the mind in its work; and the will must chose to keep the mind on its search and to desire truth.

Differentiated consciousness is essential to the work of scientists, mathematicians, logicians, lawyers, and theologians. In each of these vocations, facts or truths are sought which are not readily apparent. Each vocation requires some philosophical thought, although philosophy, as an art separate from these others, also requires the use of differentiated consciousness. They seek to discover what it is, how it is, and why it is. To know the truth becomes most important to the person functioning in differentiated consciousness. If a statement, thought, opinion, or theory does not contain a significant amount of truth, it is rejected.[63] The changes in the understanding of the subject in question are then evaluated. Some people oppose this subjective change in the realm of theology, but it prevents the perversion of the truth by false teachers.

However, all of the above are directed by the bias of an individual or a group. As different groups or generations evaluate these changes in the understanding found by others, they employ a different bias.[64] This process refines the doctrine to an enduring resonance with Scripture, observable by all cultures throughout time. Thus the development of doctrine occurs in two stages: 1) as Scripture is studied and 2) as the writings of other believers are studied in the light of Scripture.

> We may well believe that the creed only presents, in concise and partly technical language, what the Gospels imply, and that if the Gospels mean anything at all, they can only mean what the creed asserts. That is a perfectly reasonable position to adopt. . . . The Gospels afford a collection of material for theological construction; the creed puts forward inferences and conclusions based on that material. The one represents the evidence, the other records a verdict.[65]

---

63. Lonergan, *Way to Nicea*, 3.
64. Toon, *Development of Doctrine*, 110.
65. Prestige, *Fathers and Heretics*, 7.

The Basis of Theology

Usually such study happens very gradually. The significant exception to this rule occurs when a serious controversy or heresy arises; then study intensifies, debates become definitive, and truth appreciates in the eyes of the church.[66]

In addition to Scripture, worship, both individual and collective, impacts the development of doctrine.[67] As theologians participate in worship, they will become more spiritually minded.[68] Such a spiritual approach to the truth contained in Scripture is above and beyond mere differentiated consciousness. At the same time, both are necessary. As E. L. Mascall has suggested,

> The instrument which the theologian should use in performing his task is not just his rational faculty, as the post-Thomist scholastics and the Liberals have assumed, but his whole self in its sacramental union with Christ in his Mystical Body; in this, his rational powers, strengthened and illuminated by grace, will, of course, play an organic and prominent part. He is not concerned simply to make deductions from premises or to pass judgment upon the dogmas of the Faith, but to allow himself to be used by the divine head of the Mystical Body as an organ through which, in accordance with the will of God for him and for his time, some tiny fraction of the truth which is in Christ may be expressed more clearly.[69]

The Place of Tradition in Interpretation

The use of writings of other believers in developing doctrine leads to the question of how tradition should be used in interpreting Scripture. Even before the rise of postbiblical Christian writing, the church held a tradition of doctrine known as the "Rule of Faith" (*regula fidei*).[70] It was the interpretation of Scripture received from

---

66. Lonergan, *Way to Nicea*, 8–10.
67. Toon, *Development of Doctrine*, 118.
68. Mascall, *Christ, the Christian, and the Church*, 237–43.
69. Mascall, *Christ, the Christian, and the Church*, 238–39.
70. Schaff, *Creeds of Christendom*, 1:9–39. Also called the "analogy of faith"

the apostles and handed down to each succeeding generation of believers.[71] Here was the beginning of what would later be known as the orthodox interpretation—the interpretation of Scripture that best accorded with Scripture.[72] The Rule of Faith set out the uniqueness of God, the lordship of Jesus Christ, the power of the Spirit, and the place and privileges of the church.[73] The church used the Rule of Faith to detect heretical renderings of Scripture and the introduction of false doctrine, even while under persecution.[74] The effect of the rule in preserving true and pure doctrine throughout the world of the ancient church is truly remarkable. Down to the time of the first councils, faithful teachers continued to point to the Rule of Faith in the face of Gnosticism and Arianism. The rule did not replace either Scripture or serious consideration and study of Scripture. Many such serious studies from that period survive to this day, with indications that many other such studies once existed which are now lost.[75] What was not lost was the firm conviction that God had been truly revealed in Jesus Christ, whose apostles had faithfully committed his truth to his church.[76]

Here is the key: tradition is the work of fallible but faithful men. Tradition, written or oral, is not equal to the Scripture any more than other interpretations. The church must compare the traditions she receives to the Scripture itself. However, while acknowledging the human element in tradition, yet "in the multitude of counsellors *there is* safety."[77] Many proven wise men who say the same thing should be taken seriously.

> For although the sacred and inspired Scriptures are sufficient to declare the truth . . . there are other works of

---

(Blunt, "Which Bible Version?," 9) and the "canon of faith" (Kelly, *Early Christian Doctrines*, 40). See glossary for definition.

71. Irenaeus of Lyons, "Against the Heresies, III," 128–29.
72. Augustine, "On Christian Doctrine, III," 154–55.
73. Kelly, *Early Christian Doctrines*, 40–43.
74. Irenaeus of Lyons, "Against the Heresies, III," 128–29.
75. Kelly, *Early Christian Doctrines*, 46.
76. Irenaeus of Lyons, "Against the Heresies, III," 128–29.
77. Prov 11:14.

> our blessed teachers compiled for this purpose, if he meet with which a man will gain some knowledge of the interpretation of the Scriptures, and be able to learn what he wishes to know, . . . the faith, namely, of Christ the Saviour; lest any should hold cheap the doctrine taught among us, or think faith in Christ unreasonable.[78]

This enduring opinion or interpretation will keep each succeeding generation from fully accommodating its own times and culture.[79] Tradition functions as a buffer against "every wind of doctrine."[80] It also acts as a signpost or a bearing for orienteering, allowing changes to be perceived.

Those whose work became tradition labored in the word and doctrine. They should, therefore, receive double honor.[81] Their thoughts and words should not be lightly esteemed. Theirs is a fatherly wisdom and advice; the neglect of which produced the dreadful consequences that had been outlined in the book of Proverbs long before.[82] As under-shepherds, the fathers of the church watched for the souls committed to their charge, both in their own day and the children to come.[83]

Enlightenment View of Tradition

During the Enlightenment, tradition became despised due to post-Reformation pride. Many people assumed that their new era was more clever, more advanced than the older eras.[84] Antiquity became a bit of a joke. Oddly enough, much of tradition was rejected merely for its age without any consideration for its relative merit.[85]

---

78. Athanasius, "Against the Heathen," 4.
79. Kelly, *Early Christian Doctrines*, 47.
80. Eph 4:14.
81. 1 Tim 5:17.
82. Prov 5:12–14.
83. Heb 13:17; Ps 78:3–7.
84. May, *Enlightenment in America*, xiv.
85. Chesterton, *Orthodoxy*, 53.

Irrational behavior stands out all the more strongly in an age consumed with the rational.

Other parts of tradition were rejected due to their close proximity to those parts of Scripture that were deemed in need of adjustment to modern scientific thought.[86] "And yet nothing is more unreasonable than to submit the truth of God to the judgment of men, whose acuteness and sagacity amounts to nothing more than mere vanity."[87]

An element of the reaction to tradition was a subtle move on the part of philosophers. First directed against the Roman church, it was hailed by Protestant theologians until they discovered to their horror that the same arguments were used against any and all faith as faith.[88] Once sluicegates are open, they are very hard to close. Thus the tide of heresy and agnosticism not only rose at an alarming rate, it also exerted a tremendous amount of pressure. In frantically trying to combat the foes appearing on every side, most, though not all, Protestants forgot that the problem began with ignoring the Reformers' balanced approach to tradition.

Tradition in the Reformation

In 1517, Martin Luther wrote to Matthew Lang, "Our theology and St. Augustine are beginning to prosper."[89] All of the major continental Reformers had emphasized their continuity with the ancient writers.[90] They had repeated again and again that theirs was no novel interpretation of Scripture, often quoting the church fathers to prove their point.[91] The church had strayed from its own tradition, the doctrine received from the apostles. For example, no bishop of

---

86. Wiles, *Making of Christian Doctrine*, 14.

87. Calvin, *Commentary on a Harmony*, 2:18.

88. Pelikan, *Bach among the Theologians*, 50–51; cf. May, *Enlightenment in America*, 10.

89. Spitz, *Renaissance and Reformation Movements*, 2:348.

90. Spitz, *Renaissance and Reformation Movements*, 2:417; see also Pelikan, *Bach among the Theologians*, 119.

91. "French Confession of Faith, 1559," 146; "Second Helvetic Confession, 1566," 226.

The Basis of Theology

the fifteenth and sixteenth centuries was preaching on how each member of his congregation was to read and interpret Scripture in private devotion as had the Bishop of Hippo, Augustine.[92] The Reformers also believed in using the Rule of Faith.[93]

> This holy, divine Scripture is to be interpreted in no other way than out of itself and is to be explained by the rule of faith and love.
>
> ... Where the holy fathers and early teachers, who have explained and expounded the Scripture, have not departed from this rule, we want to recognize and consider them not only as expositors of Scripture, but as elect instruments through whom God has spoken and operated.[94]

While the Reformers declared that only Scripture possessed life-giving truth (*Sola Scriptura*), they referred all critics and inquirers to the ecumenical creeds as the basic statement of their faith, especially on points such as the deity of Christ and the doctrine of the Holy Trinity.[95] The Protestant confessions and catechisms for the most part relate and affirm the doctrine of the Trinity as it is found in the creeds and formulas developed and maintained by the church ecumenically and historically. Various Reformed confessions, such as the First Confession of Basel, 1534, and the First Helvetic Confession of 1536, border on stating the doctrine in ante-Nicene phraseology.[96] Others simply declare that they hold to traditional orthodoxy. Some go so far as to make a point of their steadfast hold on the historic, universal orthodox teaching regarding the Holy Trinity.[97] The Formula of Concord, 1576, declares,

> And inasmuch as immediately after the times of the Apostles, nay, even while they were yet alive, false teachers

92. Augustine, "On Christian Doctrine, III," 154–55.
93. Calvin, *Commentary on a Harmony*, 1:365.
94. "First Helvetic Confession of Faith of 1536," 100–1.
95. "First Helvetic Confession of Faith of 1536," 146; "Heidelberg Catechism, 1536," 308; see also "Augsburg Confession, A.D. 1530," 3–73.
96. Cochrane, *Reformed Confessions of the Sixteenth Century*, 89–111.
97. "Belgic Confession of Faith, 1561," 194–95.

and heretics arose, against whom in the primitive Church symbols were composed, that is to say, brief and explicit confessions, which contain the unanimous consent of the Catholic Christian faith, and the confession of the orthodox and true Church (such as are the APOSTLES', the NICENE, and the ATHANASIAN creeds); we publicly profess that we embrace them and reject all heresies and all dogmas which have ever been brought into the Church of God contrary to their decision.[98]

In this they had a credible basis from which to argue for a more biblical teaching of grace and Christ's redeeming and sanctifying work. The Reformers even employed the philosophical arguments of the ancient fathers. This, however, raises yet another question: What place does philosophy have in theology and in the interpretation of Scripture?

The Place of Philosophy in Theology

To understand the place of philosophy in the interpretation of Scripture, philosophy must first be defined. Philosophy is the application of man's reason (collectively) to premises derived from various sources. To the degree that the premises conform to God's truth and reason is correctly applied, the philosophy will be sound or, in other words, of high quality. Therefore, philosophy and reason can be treated as virtually synonymous, except where some man's "reason" is distinctly inferior to sound philosophy. Thus a philosophy can be of any level of quality and on any number of subjects. Philosophy is an interpretation of a subject; hence, philosophy of religion, philosophy of history, philosophy of science, philosophy of sociology, etc. Even within a subject or discipline more than one philosophy may exist (at times) with equal or varying worth.[99]

Theology itself employs philosophical methods. This statement may seem radical in the face of the many works regarding the relation, interface, or antagonism between philosophy and theology;

---

98. "Formula of Concord, A.D. 1576," 94–95.
99. Toon, *Development of Doctrine*, 113–14.

The Basis of Theology

but theology is the result of man's thought about God. As Augustine of Hippo wrote, "I am inviting you to a philosophy which offers to demonstrate to her true lovers this import of most copious doctrines—an import which has been divinely proclaimed, but which is ever so remote from the intellect of the profane."[100] Both good and bad theologies organize truth about God into a system of thought. However, those thoughts are not of themselves theology.[101]

> Theology is not a simple application of philosophy to revealed data—as many have thought since the time of Descartes. Were this so it would involve submitting the content of faith to human judgment and discernment. Theology is a *habitus* of wisdom rooted in faith: hence it is radically and virtually supernatural, and hence it uses philosophical knowledge as its instrument and judges it in its own light.[102]

As noted above, some systems remain closer to Scripture for their premises than do others. Others include extrabiblical premises, whether natural or experiential. Some theologians apply better logic to the premises drawn from Scripture than do others. Few who, like Augustine of Hippo, use philosophy realize with him the risks of philosophy itself.[103]

Indeed what is the proper place of logic in the interpretation of Scripture for the development of theology? The Enlightenment thinkers obviously placed great emphasis on logic and reason in theology. At times their reason went so far as to remake the premise Scripture.[104] Does reverence for Scripture conflict with logical thought? Would it not be better to set aside all thought and bow mindlessly to revelation? Indeed not and for two important considerations.

First and foremost is the divine command, central to all the law and the prophets, that man love God with all his mind.[105] "A

---

100. Augustine, "Answer to Skeptics," 104.
101. Mascall, *Christ, the Christian, and the Church*, 228–30.
102. Maritain, *Science and Wisdom*, 113.
103. Augustine, "Happy Life," 43–49.
104. Calvin, *Commentary on a Harmony*, 2:28.
105. Matt 22:37–40.

thinking Church, a Church that professes to love God with all its mind as well as with all its heart, cannot be content to lie for ever in an intellectual fallow."[106] Service and worship of God require that the believer use his head, none excepted, to whatever degree of intellect he has been endowed. "For if there be first a willing mind, *it is* accepted according to that a man hath, *and* not according to that he hath not."[107] Mindless service is no improvement on heartless service.[108] "The affections may be regarded individually as ... members: but as they are blind in themselves, they need direction. Now, God has given reason to guide them, and to act the part of a *lantern* in showing them the way."[109] No one can please God without applying diligent thought, especially in the area of doctrine. Scripture will indeed reveal man's thoughts for what they are.[110] Hence none need fear his own susceptibility to error when he humbly compares his thoughts with Scripture.

The second consideration is simply that as the Spirit opens a believer's understanding in light of Scripture, interpretation will inevitably follow: theology just happens.

> My son, if thou wilt receive my words, and hide my commandments with thee; so that thou incline thine ear unto wisdom, *and* apply thine heart to understanding; yea, if thou criest after knowledge, *and* liftest up thy voice for understanding; if thou seekest her as silver, and searchest for her as *for* hid treasures; then shalt thou understand the fear of the Lord, and find the knowledge of God. For the Lord giveth wisdom: out of his mouth cometh knowledge and understanding.[111]

As noted concerning the development of doctrine from interpretation, the teaching of Scripture requires interpretation through a human instrument. As the apostle Paul said, "Till I come, give

---

106. Prestige, *Fathers and Heretics*, 7–8.
107. 2 Cor 8:12.
108. Mark 12:29–30.
109. Calvin, *Commentary on a Harmony*, 1:335; italics original.
110. Heb 4:12.
111. Prov 2:1–6.

The Basis of Theology

attendance to reading, to exhortation, to doctrine."[112] That is how the church is designed,[113] to bear God's truth in earthly vessels.[114]

Some have objected to the use of philosophy in formulating and teaching doctrine. These people do not appreciate philosophical methods or specialized terminology in the creeds.[115] To them such methods and terminology represent the importation of man's thinking into God's truth. They appear to miss those places where they themselves interpret Scripture. The simple choosing of quotations from Scripture indicates an interpretation position, whether or not it is a good position.

Notwithstanding, Christians should teach the truth as it is. A few specialized or technical phrases which must be understood chiefly by the intellect can be explained at that level to those who ordinarily function in undifferentiated consciousness.[116] If they do not completely understand after the explanation, they do not necessarily need to perceive how a thing is true in order to believe that it is true. Most importantly, perhaps, even if many Christians do not fully appreciate all parts of the creed, they all can continue to believe it in its entirety while continuing to transmit the exact truth to future generations.

The Two Categories of Philosophy

On the other hand, Christians should not accept philosophy uncritically, especially when applied to theology. Two categories of philosophy, or human thought, are described in Scripture. These touch on the manner or type of reason applied, not so much the subject to which it is applied. Regardless of the subject under consideration, only two approaches exist: the godly, spiritual approach, or the

---

112. 1 Tim 4:13.

113. 1 Tim 3:15.

114. 2 Cor 4:7.

115. Schaff, *Creeds of Christendom*, 1:9; cf. Wiles, *Making of Christian Doctrine*, 116.

116. Mascall, *Christ, the Christian, and the Church*, 42–44.

worldly, carnal approach. Each of these is a philosophy, because each approach interprets the same facts in order to understand them.

Godly philosophy measures all thought and evaluates all facts proposed in the light of scriptural revelation. In developing theology, godly philosophy is spiritually true to the text. It includes humility (owning human limits) and relying on God's Spirit. A godly philosophy acknowledges that understanding, wisdom, and prudence are required of all believers.[117] The truths of Scripture must be ingested (understanding), cogently related to one another (wisdom), and constantly applied (prudence). Still, godly philosophy is not without variation.

On the other hand, the Worldly Wiseman comes from the town of Carnal Policy.[118] Although subtle at times, in the end the pride of worldly philosophy cannot be overlooked. The premises of its system are ultimately that which is right in every man's own eyes.[119] In spiritual matters worldly philosophy relies heavily on physical, material evidence (hence, earthly and sensual). It produces superstition by creating God in man's image (hence, devilish).[120] Human nature's propensity to this type of philosophy leads to its habitual incorporation into scriptural interpretation. As Jacques Maritain observed,

> In short, we may say that the radical fault of anthropocentric humanism has been its anthropocentric quality, not its humanism.
>
> We are thus led to distinguish between two kinds of humanism: a humanism which is theocentric or truly christian [sic]; and one which is anthropocentric...[121]

Since thinking is required to theologize correctly, the results, of course, depend on how one thinks—carnally or spiritually. "But we have the mind of Christ."[122]

117. Prov 8.
118. Bunyan, *Pilgrim's Progress*, 11.
119. Judg 17:6.
120. Jas 3:15.
121. Maritain, *True Humanism*, 19.
122. 1 Cor 2:16.

Chapter 2

Definition of the Ontology of God

GOD HAS REVEALED HIS ONTOLOGY

All consideration of the sovereignty of God must begin from a correct understanding of his ontology (essence),[1] not his will or his relations to men but his being as God. Inquiries into *how* God is sovereign will be misdirected if not founded in *who* the God is that is sovereign. Otherwise no defense exists against the inroads of man's natural superstition creating God in his own image.

God's statement of his existence was and is, without exception, all that he needed to give humanity. However, because man died spiritually at the fall of Adam, he could not know God simply by this statement of existence; and God graciously granted him more revelation through his word in order to restore the human-divine fellowship.[2]

---

1. See glossary for definition.
2. Athanasius, "On the Incarnation," 46.

Sometimes the purpose or necessity of studying and teaching God's ontology is questioned.[3] The natural world pondered by men yields truth concerning God but not concerning his very nature.[4] God, not any created being in time or space, is the source of the definition of his ontology.[5] The only source for truth concerning God's ontology is prophetic revelation,[6] which culminated in the incarnation of our Lord Jesus Christ and is preserved in Holy Scripture.[7] This revelation provides the authority and creates the necessity to discuss divine ontology. How else should man dare to think about God?[8] The very attempt would be a trespass. However, in his gracious condescension, God in his word, and especially in the Word made flesh, has given man such revelation of himself as man is able to bear.

God's Declaration to Moses

The place of ontological studies of the divine nature is found in God's revelation of himself to Moses. On Mt. Sinai at two different times, God revealed his ontology to Moses. This is not the first revelation of God, for he had spoken to believers since the world began.[9] However, God specifically told Moses that the previous revelation was not complete, as indeed the best would be saved for last.[10] At the burning bush, God declared to Moses "I AM THAT I AM."[11] No clearer definition of divine ontology could exist. It is obviously not based on his relation to man or to the created order, although it is in a redemptive context. Man is dependent on

---

3. Studer, *Trinity and Incarnation*, 3.
4. Calvin, *Institutes*, 1.1.6.1.
5. Dionysius the Areopagite, "Our Knowledge of God," 43; see also Augustine, "Faith Seeking Understanding," 256.
6. Isa 48:3–7, 11–12.
7. Mascall, *Christ, the Christian, and the Church*, 241.
8. Dionysius the Areopagite, "Our Knowledge of God," 42.
9. Luke 1:70.
10. Heb 11:40; Matt 19:30.
11. Exod 3:14.

Definition of the Ontology of God

the redemptive work of God to receive any revelation at all.[12] Man knows God through redemption,[13] but redemption does not define God. Rather it opens the way for man to know God as he is, just as a relationship allows one person to know another person.

Nevertheless, the encounter at the burning bush was not the only occasion on Mt. Sinai where God revealed his ontology to Moses. After a prolonged time of communion with God during the giving of the law, Moses petitioned to see God's glory; a complete revelation of which, he learned, would overwhelm mortal man. However, Moses had progressed far enough in fellowship with God to understand that God would be pleased to further disclose himself to the adoring heart of faith.

In the marvelous occasion that followed, God more fully detailed the name by which he had named himself to Moses at the burning bush, "The Lord, The Lord God, merciful and gracious, longsuffering, and abundant in goodness and truth, keeping mercy for thousands, forgiving iniquity and transgression and sin, and that will by no means clear *the guilty*; visiting the iniquity of the fathers upon the children, and upon the children's children, unto the third and to the fourth *generation*."[14] Moses was receiving a further revelation of God's ontology.[15] At this point all Moses had seen became, not so much a support for his faith, but a test of faith. God had descended upon Mt. Sinai in fire, thunder, and smoke,[16] so that Moses himself said, "I exceedingly fear and quake."[17] The Lord's declaration of his intrinsic and consistent goodness strongly contradicted the well-accepted, age-old conception of man's religious reasoning regarding the God of fire and storm. Moses rejected the natural conclusion in favor of acting upon God's self-revelation.

Oddly enough, God continued through the prophets to declare to his people his character and nature that he had revealed

---

12. Athanasius, "On the Incarnation," 42.
13. Ps 103:7; Jer 31:34.
14. Exod 34:6–7.
15. Fretheim, *Exodus*, 299.
16. Exod 19:18.
17. Heb 12:21.

specially to Moses. Over and over God's people experienced the truth of God's nature. Their history demonstrates how the Lord is indeed "merciful and gracious."[18] When God's people comprehended his goodness, they invariably seemed to neglect his justice, until they finally declared his ways unequal.[19] Carnal reason regarding the ontology of God poses difficulties in every generation. Both the brazen rebels and also the well-meaning but mistaken believers attribute their own conceptions to God's nature.[20] They misunderstand the enscripturated revelation of God, but God continues to reveal himself. The Shepherd of Israel would yet shine forth and lead his flock into the truth about himself.[21] In "the fullness of time" came the fullness of revelation.[22]

The Incarnation of Christ

Christ is himself the fullness of revelation.[23] While Christ's incarnation was truly "for us men and for our salvation,"[24] Christ's primary mission was to reveal the Father.[25] This Christ did by living the life of the Trinity in the flesh[26] and working the works of God.[27] In 1 John, the apostle declared it impossible for one to rightly love or worship God if he does not first believe that Jesus is the Christ, God in the flesh.[28] Jesus, "Jehovah saves," saves us as Jehovah.

> It is only when we know God the Father in and through his Son who belongs to his own being as God that we may know him in any true and accurate way, that is,

18. Exod 34:6.
19. Ezek 18:29.
20. May, *Enlightenment in America*, xiv–xv.
21. Ps 80:1.
22. Gal 4:4.
23. Torrance, *Trinitarian Faith*, 3; see also Col 1:19.
24. The Nicæno-Constantinopolitan Creed; see appendix.
25. John 17.
26. Col 2:9.
27. John 5:36; 10:37–38.
28. 1 John 4:2–3.

Definition of the Ontology of God

know God strictly in accordance with his divine nature. In order to know him in that way, however, we must enter into an intimate and saving relationship with him in Jesus Christ his incarnate Son.[29]

Christ, in his life and death, corrects mistaken views of God and provides the correct way to interpret all previous and future revelations of the divine nature.[30] Thus an understanding of the doctrine of the Holy Trinity as revealed in the incarnation of our Lord Jesus Christ is as central to a proper understanding of God's sovereignty as it is to understanding any of God's operations in creation.

In Christ's life, he not only manifested the truth about the divine nature by his actions, he explained by his teachings that which his life demonstrated.[31] Much of what Christ taught reiterated Old Testament revelation. Not only do believers need repetition to learn[32] but the ways, means, and places where Christ included and interpreted Old Testament revelation also define how the revelation of God's ontology in the Old Testament is to be understood.

Indeed, all Scripture must be understood in Christ the Word,[33] the Light of men,[34] "who of God is made unto us wisdom."[35] God's dealings with believers seem to be channeled chiefly, but not exclusively, through Christ Jesus. This sometimes gives the impression that though the Father is interested in his people, they are the Son's responsibility; but the book of Philippians (not to mention the remainder of Scripture) does not bear this out. Nevertheless, in Christ, believers see most clearly God-as-God-is-toward-us. "He is, as it were, the Father's *alter ego*, the perfect image in which the Father expresses and to which he communicates everything that he himself is."[36] Christ may not be said to act alongside the Trinity, nor

---

29. Torrance, *Trinitarian Faith*, 3.
30. Basil of Caesarea, *On the Holy Spirit*, 34.
31. Athanasius, "On the Incarnation," 58.
32. Athanasius, "Against the Arians, I," 28.
33. John 1:1, 14.
34. John 1:4, 9.
35. 1 Cor 1:30.
36. Mascall, *Christ, the Christian, and the Church*, 2; italics original.

do the attributes of any of the persons of the Godhead contradict the character of God. However, both Colossians 1:18-22 and 2:9-12 indicate that believers experience the Trinity only in Christ. Every part of a believer's existence and actions is "by," "in," and "of" Christ.[37] In the New Testament particularly, believers are instructed on practical ways to look beyond their immediate physical surroundings and to live in the spiritual reality that God the Father, the Son, and the Spirit has made theirs and is working together to reveal already in their fleshly state.

> That is to say, everything that is Christ's in virtue of his sonship is ours by our adoption into him. We receive—of course in a way adapted to our mode of existence as creatures, for *quidquid recipitur recipitur ad modus recipientis*—a real participation in the life of the Holy Trinity; through our union with Christ we are caught up into the act whereby he eternally adores the heavenly Father. We are made, in the New Testament phrase, 'partakers of the divine nature.'[38]

In both books, Philippians and Colossians, God summons his people to a greater realization of who he is towards them.

Christ's teaching ministry did not end at his ascension. His spiritual presence in the life (including the teaching ministry) of the church should in no way be overlooked, especially as it is the fulfillment of his own promises.[39] Just as he promised, the revelation given through his Spirit after his resurrection and ascension has abounded to a greater degree than it did during his earthly ministry.[40] This revelation included the whole New Testament. The instruction for interpreting that revelation continues in the work of the Spirit as he opens Scripture to believers, as noted before. The individual aspects of this instruction are often better understood

---

37. Basil of Caesarea, *On the Holy Spirit*, 39.

38. Mascall, *Christ, the Christian, and the Church*, 96 (2 Pet 1:4) [Latin—"that which is received is received according to the mode of reception" (my translation)]. See also Eph 3:6 and Col 3:1, 3.

39. Augustine, "Faith Seeking Understanding," 256–57. See also Matt 28:19–20 and John 14–16.

40. Hahn, *Kinship by Covenant*, 233–37.

Definition of the Ontology of God

than the corporate effects.[41] How does the Spirit of Christ reveal Christ, and through him the Father, to the church? How has such been accomplished through the centuries following the ascension? Before examining the process that was applied and the opposition it incurred and continues to incur,[42] the nature of the Holy Trinity revealed in Christ and how it must be viewed by believers should be examined and understood.

THE TRINITY AND THE DIVINE ONTOLOGY

The Ontological and Economic[43] Views of the Trinity

What exactly is the Trinity which Christ revealed? God is the Trinity—three co-equal, co-eternal persons who are mutually indwelling each other and together one God. This Trinity is revealed to believers in Holy Scripture by the name of the Father, the Son, and the Holy Ghost.[44] Believers can only know the Trinity by direct revelation, which is found in the economy of grace[45] as taught in Scripture. God has given man a complex revelation of himself. Orthodox interpretation of that revelation is divided into two categories: the *Economic* and the *Ontological/Immanent* views of the Trinity.[46]

The Economic Trinity is the description of God's nature as it relates to man, God-as-God-is-toward-us. Not as clear as the Economic Trinity, the Immanent Trinity appears only after careful study.[47] The first view has to do with God's nature as it is evidenced in his relation to man; the other with his nature separate from any other consideration.[48] The Ontological (or Immanent) Trinity is

---

41. Basil of Caesarea, *On the Holy Spirit*, 42–44.
42. See chapters 5, 6.
43. See glossary for definitions of these terms.
44. Matt 28:19.
45. See glossary for definition.
46. Studer, *Trinity and Incarnation*, 1.
47. Toon, *Our Triune God*, 37–40. See glossary for definitions of these terms.
48. Hill, *Three-Personed God*, 50–51, 60.

the description of God's divine nature as defined by itself and its own inner workings, God-as-God-is-in-himself. The Economic Trinity is God-as-God-is-toward-us in the economy of grace.[49] The Ontological Trinity is God-as-God-is-in-himself before, during, and after this present time. The Economic Trinity, God-as-God-is-toward-us, is grounded entirely in the Ontological Trinity, God-as-God-is-in-himself.[50] These are not two trinities but two facets or ways of understanding the one Holy Trinity, which is God the Father, the Son, and the Holy Ghost. Both of these are interrelated in that there is only one God.[51]

How the two are mentally related must be consonant with the revelation that one is attempting to categorize. Both of these contemplations of God are necessary. Eternal salvation depends on how God relates to man. However, without a consideration of God's own character independent of his creation, man may not only become self-oriented, he may also develop an unscriptural view of God, which in turn can affect his salvation.[52] Man's view of God (developed on the basis of natural human perception) is a mere shadow rather than a true image of God's essence.

The Trinity is a matter of essence, not merely of perception. The doctrine of the Trinity is required by the content of the sacred text.[53] Although it is the foundation for all other doctrines and therefore involved in them, the doctrine of the Trinity, like the foundation of a building, must be rightly set in one's mind before he can proceed to a thorough investigation of the other doctrines. When men attempt to expound the other doctrines while merely assuming a vague trinitarianism within those other doctrines, they usually find themselves teaching contrary to the express statements of Scripture at some point.[54] This is proof that the doctrine of the Trinity is explicitly required by the sacred text. Those who hold the

---

49. Toon, *Our Triune God*, 43–44.
50. Toon, *Our Triune God*, 48.
51. Studer, *Trinity and Incarnation*, 1.
52. Athanasius, "On the Incarnation," 44–45; see also Torrance, *Trinitarian Faith*, 50–51.
53. Toon, *Our Triune God*, 67–68.
54. Studer, *Trinity and Incarnation*, 3.

Definition of the Ontology of God

doctrine of the Trinity as merely incorporated into all other doctrines may as well suppose that the foundation of a skyscraper is merely intrinsic in all the floors.

Yet many people do not see the doctrine of the Trinity as central.[55] In fact they appear to think it irrelevant to the practical Christian life. Most of them focus on the commandments of the New Testament: believe on Christ as Savior and then behave as God requires in order to experience a better life now and in eternity. One must remember that the concluding words of Christ before his final blessing give the designation by which God's people are to name the persons of the Trinity.[56] The religion to be proclaimed is based on the truth that God is Trinity.[57]

Beyond the simple proclamation of the Trinity in baptism and preaching, believers must realize the importance of the doctrine of the Trinity in their individual lives and in the congregation of the church.[58] Believing in Christ includes much more than routine obedience and a quality life. Each day as believers they can and should experience God as Father through the redemption and mediation of his only-begotten Son, and understand the truth of this relationship by the ministry of the Holy Spirit, which Christ said he would send from the Father. While no ranking exists in the Godhead, the Son in *his* grace toward humanity willingly humbled himself to be sent by the Father in *his* grace toward them and to be offered to the Father "through the eternal Spirit"[59] in *his* grace toward them for the pardon of their sins and for their reconciliation to God, including the incorporation of believers into the fellowship and inner life of the Holy Trinity.[60] Thus in the love proper to the Immanent Trinity, the economy of grace is exercised upon all creatures by the free, mutual counsel of the three divine persons in what is known as the Economic Trinity.

---

55. Studer, *Trinity and Incarnation*, 2–3.
56. Basil of Caesarea, *On the Holy Spirit*, 46–47, 48–50.
57. Studer, *Trinity and Incarnation*, 1.
58. Torrance, *Trinitarian Faith*, 54.
59. Heb 9:14.
60. Studer, *Trinity and Incarnation*, 9.

Earth Shadows on the Sky

God's Essence and God's Work

While to dissolve the Immanent Trinity into the Economic Trinity is dangerous, as that leads to anthropocentric soteriology, at the same time one must not try to draw too sharp of a distinction between the two.[61] Perhaps the best way to understand the two views is that the Economic Trinity may be dissolved into the Immanent Trinity.[62] The "Father of our Lord Jesus Christ"[63] describes God-as-God-is-in-himself.[64] In this mysterious relationship of the co-eternal persons of the Godhead lies the only ontological divine sonship. The title "Our Father which art in heaven"[65] describes clearly God-as-God-is-toward-us.[66] Avoiding confusion of the Economic Trinity with the Immanent Trinity is extremely difficult for many. Although they may never confuse the persons of the Godhead with each other, believers may confuse the ontological relations with the work of each of the persons as expressed in the economy of grace.[67]

God's essence is the source of his work. Whenever God's work is considered, whether it is his creation, redemption, judgment or any other work, it must be understood in light of what God has revealed of his nature or essence. Never should God's work replace or be confused with his essence as a definition of God.[68] God is not in his essence Creator, Redeemer, or Judge.[69] That each of these titles describes or identifies the works which are his sole prerogative is true, but God is a merciful Judge[70] and a faithful Creator[71] because he fulfills these roles in accordance with his nature or ontology.

---

61. Dionysius the Areopagite, "Our Knowledge of God," 45.
62. Toon, *Our Triune God*, 228–29.
63. Rom 15:6.
64. Torrance, *Trinitarian Faith*, 79.
65. Matt 6:9.
66. Toon, *Doctrine of the Trinity*.
67. Studer, *Trinity and Incarnation*, 113.
68. Basil of Caesarea, *On the Holy Spirit*, 35.
69. Torrance, *Trinitarian Faith*, 52.
70. Gen 18:25; Exod 34:6; Ps 86:3, 5.
71. 1 Pet 4:19.

Definition of the Ontology of God

In his essence as Trinity, God creates, redeems, and judges.[72] That much Scripture makes evident.[73] God's sovereignty is exercised not in tri-part delegation, but in triunity.[74] Therefore, since salvation and judgment are mediated through Christ,[75] how Christ relates to the Godhead as a whole has profound implications for that salvation and judgment. Although fully revealed in the New Testament, the full outworking of those implications was to be the Spirit's work in the church.

---

72. Toon, *Our Triune God*, 37.

73. Scripture references showing each member of the Trinity acting in creation include: Gen 1:3, the Father; John 1:1, 3, the Son; and Gen 1:2, the Spirit. Scripture references showing each member of the Trinity acting in redemption include: John 3:16, the Father; 1 Pet 3:18, the Son; and Heb 9:14, the Spirit. Scripture references showing each member of the Trinity judging include: John 8:16, the Father; John 5:22, the Son; and John 16:7–8, 11, the Spirit.

74. Torrance, *Trinitarian Faith*, 52.

75. For example: salvation (1 Thess 5:9; 2 Tim 2:10; Heb 2:10; 5:9) and judgment (Acts 10:42; Rom 2:16).

Chapter 3

Development of the Orthodox Doctrine of God's Ontology

EARLY TRIUNE STATEMENTS

Confessions of the Faith

The faith of the early church was simple, but it was also trinitarian from the very beginning.[1] Such a trinitarian structure was natural because Christ's final instruction to the apostles declared that they were to baptize "in the name of the Father, and of the Son, and of the Holy Ghost."[2] The apostle Paul also indicates that confession of all three persons was and is necessary at baptism.[3] Therefore, that the earliest known trinitarian formulae should be baptismal confessions is not surprising. These confessions of the faith were the bases

---

1. Hill, *Three-Personed God*, 3.
2. Matt 28:19.
3. Acts 19:1–5.

Development of the Orthodox Doctrine of God's Ontology

of the later creeds.[4] A convert declared which faith he believed and professed by his baptism. "This baptismal faith always remained the central core of the Church's proclamation, and constantly formed the centre of Christian theology. The baptismal creed, given to all baptismal candidates, developed out of this, as well as the *regula fidei*, on which all theological endeavor was founded."[5]

The first baptismal creed to gain widespread acceptance eventually formed the Apostles' Creed.[6] The Apostles' Creed, said to be thus named because it contains the basic teachings of the apostles, uses only words of Scripture.[7] Although the early church lacked philosophically technical terms, it held tenaciously to Scripture. Most importantly, the faith of the early church was expressed in vital, believable teaching.[8] The Apostles' Creed in particular records the Trinity as it is known in the economy of grace. The Father is known in creation; the Son in the incarnation; and the Spirit in the church. Yet in devoting a paragraph to each of the three persons, the creed gives equal glory to each.

> It may be presupposed that a knowledge of faith in the Trinity was expected of the baptismal candidates from an early stage, and that it was therefore felt necessary to compile for them the doctrine of the three names, i.e. of the three articles of faith. This was given extended treatment in the so-called *regulae fidei* and more summary treatment in the creed.[9]

Thus true doctrine was preserved in its entirety, though not in depth.

The structure of the Apostles' Creed is reflected in later creeds which include a more thoroughly developed doctrine of the

---

4. Norris, "I Believe in God," 21.

5. Studer, *Trinity and Incarnation*, 240.

6. See chapter 1 of Quasten, *Patrology*, vol. 1, for an overview of the history and the debates surrounding the development of this creed.

7. *Catholic* and *universalem* are each correct Latin translations of the Greek word translated "general" in the Authorized (King James) Version of Heb 12:23.

8. Hill, *Three-Personed God*, 7.

9. Studer, *Trinity and Incarnation*, 29.

Earth Shadows on the Sky

Trinity.[10] The Nicene Creed and its expansion, the Niceno-Constantinopolitan Creed, do not significantly alter either the structure of the Apostles' Creed or its phraseology.

While no evidence is extant that the church had any need at this stage to expound or explain the relations of the persons of the Trinity to each other, nevertheless one should not overlook that those who confessed Jesus to be the Son of God[11] and Lord of all[12] were making cogent assertions regarding the relation of the Son to the Father.[13] At first these statements correctly defining the relation of Jesus Christ to God the Father and to believers remained unassailed; no further explanation was necessary.

While finding the earliest trinitarian statements not surprising in baptismal confessions, discovering that these confessions were almost solely economic in focus is not surprising either.[14] The baptism of repentance would most certainly be bound up with salvation. As the apostle Peter indicated, the believers were baptized as the Lord Jesus Christ had commanded because their sins had been forgiven.[15] Hence the focus would be on grace ministered to man from the Father through the Son by the Spirit. This is undoubtedly the correct approach of faith and worship for any believer as outlined in the New Testament.[16] Such must not be confused with the defining of God's essence by his works. God is to be praised and worshipped in and for his work of grace, not defined by it. Christ is the Mediator of the new covenant[17] and the way to God.[18] This is largely the central message of the whole of Scripture and how believers enter the life of the Trinity.[19] As these truths are compre-

---

10. Torrance, *Christian Doctrine of God*, 79.
11. Acts 8:37.
12. Acts 10:36.
13. Quasten, *Patrology*, 1:24–25.
14. Studer, *Trinity and Incarnation*, 29, 61.
15. Acts 2:38; Matt 28:19–20.
16. Toon, *Our Triune God*, 223–28.
17. Heb 12:24.
18. John 14:6.
19. See chapter 2.

hended and applied, the believer embraces the right view of God and of himself.[20]

Truths that vital are worth living and dying for. Consequently, another type of confession came into existence: the martyr confessions. Those on trial for their loyalty to Christ had to declare their beliefs in short, concise statements; and just as Christ had promised, in the hour of legal trial believers were given what to say.[21] The fulfillment of this promise is evident in the poetic beauty and spiritual power of the recorded martyrs' confessions. For example,

> St. Epipodius of Lyons (+ 178): '*Christus cum Patre et Spiritu Sancto Deum esse confiteor, dignumque est, ut illi* [*scil. Christo*] *animam meam refundam, qui mihi et creator est et redemptor*—I confess Christ to be God, with the Father and the Holy Ghost, and it is meet that I should give back my soul to Him [i.e., Christ], Who is my Creator and Redeemer.' The holy deacon Vincent, who died a martyr's death, A.D. 304, is reported to have professed his faith in these words: '*Dominum Christum confiteor, Filium altissimi Patris, unici unicum, ipsum cum Patre et Spiritu Sancto unum solum Deum esse profiteor*—I confess the Lord Jesus Christ, Son of the most high Father, the Only One of the Only One, I confess Him with the Father and the Holy Ghost to be the one sole God.' To St. Euplus of Catania (+ 304) we owe one of the most beautiful confessions of faith in the Trinity that has come down to us from the early days. It is as follows: '*Patrem et Filium et Spiritum Sanctum adoro; sanctam Trinitatem adoro, praeter quam non est Deus. . . . Sacrifico modo Christo Deo meipsum. . . . Ego sacrifico et immolo meipsum Patri et Filio et Spiritui Sancto*—I adore the Father and the Son and the Holy Ghost; I adore the holy Trinity, besides which there is no God. . . . I now sacrifice myself to Christ, [who is] God; . . . I sacrifice and immolate myself to the Father, and to the Son, and to the Holy Ghost.'[22]

---

20. Augustine, *Trinity*, 28–29.
21. Matt 10:17–20.
22. Pohle, *Divine Trinity*, 137–39; italics original.

Facing the vain and arrogant assertions of man's sovereignty, the martyrs countered with the royal majesty of all three persons of the Godhead, especially that person most decried, the Lord Jesus Christ. In light of the pagan attacks on the person of Christ, the martyr confessions are, of necessity, ontological in nature. The Christ they served was God, as was the Father.[23] While their declarations about the Spirit are not as pointed regarding his divinity, they leave little room to doubt that these faithful Christians realized that the Spirit was above all created beings.[24]

These martyr confessions serve to complete the picture of what the early Christian church believed about the Trinity. The church appears to have perceived from Scripture the ontology of God and therefore of each of the persons in the Godhead, although their exact relations to each other remained to be defined.[25] Within the process of defining the intra-relation of the Trinity, the church risked forfeiting some of the truth she already knew regarding the essence of God.[26] Such a dangerous process might seem to be better avoided, but that was not the case. The worshipping church was designed to grow, and as perilous as the process of growth may be, its blessed result would be doctrine for mature believers.

Pastoral Writings

Part of the development process that would lead to the mature dogma of the Holy Trinity included the pastoral writings of those teachers and pastors who would later be known as the church fathers. Most of these writings were didactic. Some are transcriptions of sermons or catechismal lectures. Others are letters or books written to teach Christian truths, especially to expound Scripture. As might be expected, these writings center on the Economic view of the Trinity. Not all of these are on soteriology; many relate to God's

---

23. Studer, *Trinity and Incarnation*, 18–19.
24. Basil of Caesarea, *On the Holy Spirit*, 45–47.
25. Studer, *Trinity and Incarnation*, 21.
26. Gregory of Nazianzus, *Faith Gives Fullness to Reasoning*, 293–94.

Development of the Orthodox Doctrine of God's Ontology

work in and for the individual believer and for the church.[27] Since the edification of the believers is in grace and knowledge,[28] didactic writings needed to be primarily concerned with the economy of grace.

When in the second half of the third century doctrinal developments began to intensify (as distinct from presenting the faith or refuting heresies), the focus was naturally on the person of Christ as he was to be understood by the faithful. Rooted in the initial believing experience and expounded as the basis for all other beliefs, this focus on Christ brought about the christological controversies in full force as soon as Christianity was legalized.[29]

Of a somewhat different nature were the polemic writings. These were designed to warn believers of error and to rebuke the gainsayers.[30] Even while the canon of Scripture was being penned, heresies arose in the church.[31] Part of championing the truth included, though to a lesser degree, fighting errors, of which the primary and most dangerous errors pertained to the person of Christ. While the martyrs upheld Christ to the pagan persecutors, the fathers upheld Christ to the heretics who would deny some aspect of the incarnation or would introduce bizarre teachings regarding the nature of the entire Godhead.[32] As time went on, fewer heresies and strange doctrines were propounded concerning the nature of God as God. Instead, the controversy began to increasingly center on the person of Christ, especially in his relation to the Father.[33] The polemic writings, therefore, were largely focused on the ontology of God and the place of Christ in the Trinity.[34] Unfortunately, the erroneous doctrines of the christological controversy were much more difficult to combat because they were not as bizarre as the

---

27. Studer, *Trinity and Incarnation*, 23.
28. 2 Pet 3:18.
29. Calhoun, *Scripture, Creed, Theology*, 207–26.
30. Titus 1:9–14.
31. 1 Cor 11:19; Gal 5:20; 2 Pet 2:1.
32. Studer, *Trinity and Incarnation*, 19.
33. Hägglund, *History of Theology*, 75.
34. Quasten, *Patrology*, 2:105–6, 2:114–15.

former heresies. These errors were more subtle because their argument came from perverse renderings of Scripture.[35] How much more when they also incorporated the most accepted philosophy?

> When the Christian Gospel was proclaimed in that context [of the Graeco-Roman civilization], very quickly a sharp conflict emerged . . . between a mythological way of thinking (μυθολογεῖν) from a centre in the human mind and a theological way of thinking (θεολογεῖν) from a centre in God. In particular, the biblical teaching about God's providential and saving activity in history, and the Christian message of incarnation and redemption in space and time, had to struggle with the underlying assumptions of a dualist outlook upon God and the world in order to be heard aright and take root.[36]

THE ARIAN CONTROVERSY

Arian Ontological Errors

Such an opponent was Arianism. Arius proposed that the Christian doctrine which he had been taught fit perfectly into Middle Platonism, or perhaps he read scriptural truth through the filter of the platonic mindset within which he lived. He and his supporters assumed that the current Greek philosophy could not only help them to understand God in philosophical terms, but also that the Greek system was completely correct.[37]

The Greeks believed that all that existed could and ought to be explained. Following the assumption that man's reason could discover a solution to any apparent difficulty, Arius and his followers insisted on applying Hellenistic reasoning to the doctrine of God.[38] Since the concepts of divine uniqueness and of three distinguishable beings, all of whom were called "God" seemed to contradict

---

35. Fortman, *Triune God*, 64.
36. Torrance, *Trinitarian Faith*, 47–48.
37. Wiles, *Making of Christian Doctrine*, 33.
38. Studer, *Trinity and Incarnation*, 18.

Development of the Orthodox Doctrine of God's Ontology

each other, Arius took the teachings of the church and arranged them to the point of denying some in order that all could be humanly understandable.[39]

In attempting to fit Christianity into Hellenistic philosophy, Arianism assumed that certain Christian principles are true and that certain Neoplatonic principles are true.[40] Arius taught that the Holy Trinity was comprised of three utterly distinct beings. The Father, according to Arius, was a Monad and the only being who could properly be called God. The Son, also called the Logos, was created by the Father out of nothing before the ages.[41] The created order could not bear the weight of direct contact with the increate; therefore, God created the Word, his Son, to create the world.[42] The Spirit was then created to assist the Son.[43]

Arius expressly taught that the Son was inferior to the Father.[44] While various forms of Arianism would differ as to what extent and in what manner the Son was inferior to the Father, the subordination of the Son remained the main tenet of Arianism.[45] Arius developed his views by assuming that certain Neoplatonic propositions about the ontology of God were correct, and then reading the Scriptures through the lens of these propositions.[46] He and his followers quickly seized on all Scripture texts that express Christ's humiliation and submission to the Father.[47] These texts seem to agree with the Platonic view of an intermediary being between God and man. As Basil of Caesarea wrote, "The source of this distinction of theirs is pagan philosophy, but they do not always precisely follow the system."[48] Arianism assumed Christ had some obligation to cre-

39. Torrance, *Trinitarian Faith*, 118.
40. Quasten, *Patrology*, 3:8.
41. Torrance, *Trinitarian Faith*, 118.
42. Quasten, *Patrology*, 3:8.
43. Basil of Caesarea, *On the Holy Spirit*, 21–22.
44. Fortman, *Triune God*, 69.
45. Gregory of Nazianzus, *Faith Gives Fullness to Reasoning*, 245–78.
46. Basil of Caesarea, *On the Holy Spirit*, 19–22.
47. Gregory of Nazianzus, *Faith Gives Fullness to Reasoning*, 262–73. See also Alexander of Alexandria, "Epistles on the Arian Heresy," 294.
48. Basil of Caesarea, *On the Holy Spirit*, 21.

ation. He was responsible to save his creation; perhaps he was even brought into being by the Father in eternity past for the purpose of creating and then saving the creation.[49] He may have possibly made an agreement with the Father for that purpose when he came into being.[50] The Arians styled Christ's work as Mediator the entire sum and purpose of his essence and existence.[51]

Arianism threatened Christianity by using selected parts of Scripture with an attractive philosophical system. This involved manipulating Christian expressions by assigning different meanings to each one,[52] making Christianity appear to coincide neatly with the prevailing culture instead of setting the church against the world. It also meant elevating the doctrine of soteriology above Christology.

Soteriological Focus of Arianism

Arianism focused almost exclusively on soteriology, even though its propositions were framed in ontological terms.[53] Man's salvation was for the Arians the whole point of divine revelation; otherwise God would have remained alone. Christ had been created, they claimed, to manage the Father's creation, including exemplifying to mankind how to approach God by living a life of perfect obedience to the point of death. By imitating Jesus and employing his services of intercession, man could be reconciled to God and become a son of God, just like Jesus.[54] While the Father's generous gift of the Spirit made Jesus the Christ, and while Jesus would always be greater than any believer, he continued to be considered *primus par intres* (the first among fellows). For each of these assertions the Arians could produce Scripture texts. For those Scriptures that were brought against their interpretation, they redefined the words to

49. Fortman, *Triune God*, 64.
50. Basil of Caesarea, *On the Holy Spirit*, 40.
51. Calhoun, *Scripture, Creed, Theology*, 229–30.
52. Fortman, *Triune God*, 69.
53. Fortman, *Triune God*, 64–65.
54. This teaching of Arianism is documented in its refutation by Alexander of Alexandria, "Epistles on the Arian Heresy," 292.

Development of the Orthodox Doctrine of God's Ontology

accommodate their theories.[55] To the common believer, the Arians seemed to have a conclusive argument. After all, it appeared to come from Scripture and to be sensible.[56]

Rational Basis of Arianism

The problem was, of course, that the Arian teachings did not agree with all of Scripture. Certain portions had to be reread with revised definitions in order to force them into the Arian framework.[57] The explanation for this is that the framework was built on human reasoning and pagan philosophy. Scripture was used as a secondary support. "Arius was concerned to develop a theology that will appeal to the mind of a fully trained modern man. He considers himself a spokesman for the Christian doctrine that can meet the tests of students and not merely appeal to the ignorant."[58] Arius reasoned that since God was pure and man was evil, God could have no direct contact with man. Therefore, the one who managed and redeemed the fallen creation could not have been God in the absolute sense. Perhaps he was a lesser god or later became God, but the Arians would not admit that Christ was eternally God.[59]

The orthodox were exceedingly concerned to defend the deity of Christ; however, they realized that other Christian doctrines also suffered as a result of the Arian heresy. For instance, the doctrine of man was treated by the Arians as if sinners could of their own ability please God. Ironically, the soteriological focus of Arianism caused the greatest dilemma in the doctrine of salvation. If Christ was not fully God, how could he fully reconcile man to God? How could any created being, of whatever state of exaltation, offer an atonement acceptable to an infinitely holy God? If man could imitate the life of Christ with a little assistance, why did he need salvation at all?

---

55. Athanasius, "Defense of the Nicene Council," 162–64.
56. Hanson, *Search for the Christian Doctrine of God*, 128.
57. Fortman, *Triune God*, 69.
58. Calhoun, *Scripture, Creed, Theology*, 231.
59. Augustine, *Trinity*, 19.

The fathers of the conciliar period (*circa* AD 300–500) were far from being unconcerned or dispassionate regarding soteriology.[60] Although Christology and the doctrine of the Trinity were paramount in their thought, soteriology was never disjointed from theology. They were theocentric because God's honor and glory (which included Christ's honor and glory) were first, while man's salvation was secondary in their teaching. They loved God foremost and then their neighbor as themselves.[61] Hence, Arianism was a twofold offense: against Christ's dignity as God and also against their own souls and those of their flocks.[62] Wading amid the doctrinal havoc, the orthodox bishops strove to discover some method to preserve the teaching of truth.

ACHIEVEMENT AT NICAEA

Use of Scripture and the Rule of Faith

The answer, of course, was Scripture itself. The truth of God is found only in Scripture. The orthodox did not try to defend Scripture as such: that truth could stand on its own, and they, in turn, could stand on it. Indeed, Peter Toon itemizes the Scriptures which support the creedal declarations regarding each person of the Holy Trinity.[63] Rather, these orthodox bishops earnestly desired to prevent the radical redefinition of Scripture. To this end they relied on tradition and the *regula fidei*, the Rule of Faith. The Council of Nicaea reexamined Scripture with meticulous care, comparing "spiritual things with spiritual."[64] They concluded that what they had been taught through the *regula fidei* was truly the teaching of the apostles as preserved in Scripture. The Nicene Fathers demonstrated that orthodox doctrine was formulated from the image of God as received from above rather than reflected onto God from below. The fathers had indeed

---

60. Wiles, *Making of Christian Doctrine*, 62.
61. Matt 22:37–40.
62. Torrance, *Trinitarian Faith*, 116.
63. Toon, *Our Triune God*, 133–93.
64. 1 Cor 2:13.

handed down the correct interpretation of Scripture that could still be defended from Scripture. "That is to say, this Creed, while in its final form ecumenical, represents an outgrowth of an original Baptismal Creed of an ancient and venerated Church."[65] Creeds are sometimes called definitions,[66] which name can be beneficial as it elucidates both their use and manner of development.

Use of Philosophy

> In its struggle with the prevailing dualist assumptions that distorted understanding of its message, the Church found it had to transform the very foundations of Graeco-Roman thought, and in so doing it laid the basis for a very different approach to the created universe. . . . Critical and reconstructive work of this kind called for strenuous intellectual activity in the Church during the first six centuries, which has left a permanent mark upon western civilisation, but it was subsidiary to its main missionary task in evangelising the world, disseminating among the nations the saving knowledge of God mediated through Jesus Christ his Son, and providing the people of God throughout history with an articulate grasp of the substance of the Faith.[67]

Although many have asserted, or repeated the assertion, that the Greek fathers and the councils they convened corrupted the gospel with Greek metaphysics,[68] no serious attempt has ever been made to prove that the ancient Greek ecumenical creeds are actually unscriptural, either in basis or in final form. On the other hand, in spite of these assertions, the ecumenical creeds have been found to resonate with Scripture by those from non-Hellenistic philosophies. While numerous authors have demonstrated the scriptural basis of those creeds, still others have recognized the scriptural truth of the

---

65. Bishop, *Development of Trinitarian Doctrine*, 13.
66. Kelly, *Early Christian Doctrines*, 339.
67. Torrance, *Trinitarian Faith*, 48.
68. Bishop, *Development of Trinitarian Doctrine*, 24.

final forms of the creeds.[69] The reason for this scriptural finish, as well as the scriptural foundation, is found in the frequent and steady examination and reexamination of the logical and philosophical steps in the formation of the creedal statements by the light of the Scriptures, both individually and collectively. They believed that "the precise meaning of theological terms is to be found in their actual use under the transforming impact of divine revelation."[70]

Much of the disapproval of the Nicene Creed in particular comes from the incorporation of nonscriptural words.[71] As noted above, the inclusion of these words was the last resort of the Nicene bishops. Yet they did resort to these terms that had long been used to guard the *regula fidei* and with good cause.[72]

> It was recognized by Athanasius and the Nicene fathers that they could not but make use of human images and analogies in seeking to express their understanding of the relation of the Son to the Father, for that is how divine revelation has been mediated to us in and through human language. Taken by themselves these images and analogies are unsatisfactory and so they may not be pressed, but they are nevertheless employed by divine revelation with an admirable exactness in being made to point beyond their creaturely content to what God discloses of his own inner divine relations.[73]

The key to knowing whether the Nicene Creed contains pagan Greek philosophy or only Greek philosophical technique is to examine how the words *ousia* (especially in its derivative *homoousios*) and *hypostasis*[74] are employed. No one can use any word with his own definition without developing that definition. The various Greek philosophers did develop various connotations for

---

69. Wainwright, "Foreword," x.

70. Torrance, *Christian Doctrine of God*, 117.

71. This has been since the creed was first written. See Gregory of Nazianzus, *Faith Gives Fullness to Reasoning*, 290–95.

72. Studer, *Trinity and Incarnation*, 70–85.

73. Torrance, *Trinitarian Faith*, 120.

74. See glossary for definition.

Development of the Orthodox Doctrine of God's Ontology

these words within their individual systems.[75] To be understood the creed had to use these words in one or another of their current connotations. However, the context of the words is radically different from any Greek philosopher.[76] If anyone should attempt to read the definition of any Greek philosophy into either of these words, the Nicene Creed would be self-contradictory. "If God is in himself what he is in the person and activity of his incarnate Word and Son, then the being of *ousia* (οὐσία) of God must be understood in a very un-Greek way."[77]

The use of *homoousios* was intended to make the orthodox teaching regarding the deity of Christ perfectly clear.

> The explicit formulation of the *homoousion* at the Council of Nicaea was an absolutely fundamental event that took place in the mind of the early Church. It was a decisive step in deeper understanding of the Gospel, giving precise expression to the all-important relation between the incarnate Son and God the Father, which they made in obedience to God's saving revelation in Jesus Christ and in continuity with the apostolic tradition upon which the Church could not go back. With it a giant step was taken in grasping and giving expression to the internal relation of the incarnate Son to the Father, and thereby to the ontological substructure and coherence of the Gospel.[78]

This expression could not possibly be twisted to agree with the Arian teaching. Translated into Latin and English as "consubstantial," this expression confirmed that the Son has an identical essence with the Father.[79] It maintained the correct interpretation of the Scriptures which Arius had wrested. *Homoousios* provided faithful believers with a concrete answer to Arian subtleties.[80] The development of

---

75. Fortman, *Triune God*, 67; see also Studer, *Trinity and Incarnation*, 43.
76. Torrance, *Trinitarian Faith*, 129.
77. Torrance, *Trinitarian Faith*, 131.
78. Torrance, *Christian Doctrine of God*, ix–x.
79. Fortman, *Triune God*, 67–72.
80. Studer, *Trinity and Incarnation*, 104–5.

this definition was one reason the creed was viewed as daring and revolutionary.

The truth is that one cannot employ "street language" to expound the mysteries of God. The *homoousios* of the Nicene Creed was a development in doctrine from one kind of clarity to another, from undifferentiated to differentiated consciousness. The bishops present at the council did not formulate a new and unheard-of teaching. Instead, they developed a more precise manner to state the faith taught by Scripture and defined by those who had been in Christ before them.[81] "In the perspective of the Nicene faith in Jesus Christ, the true and eternal Son of God, it became possible to view the relationship between Father and Son in purely theological [ontological] terms, without considering his mediatorship in creation and salvation."[82] Therefore, while the creed may indeed contain a Greek philosophical technique, it employs scriptural wisdom instead of pagan Greek philosophy.[83]

> Thus through their exegetical and theological activity the Nicene fathers came up with the all-important ὁμοούσιος τῷ Πατρί which brought to decisive expression the ontological substructure upon which the evangelical message of the New Testament about Jesus Christ rested and in terms of which its various writings could be integrated in accordance with their saving import.[84]

In addition to the composition of the creed, the orthodox responded to the Arians' misinterpretation of Scripture by using many more Scripture passages in their liturgies in order to guard the meaning of Scripture by Scriptures that referred to the equality of the three persons of the Trinity.[85] "It should have become quite clear that in the final analysis the mystery of Father, Son and Spirit reveals itself

---

81. Rom 16:7.

82. Studer, *Trinity and Incarnation*, 113; see also Torrance, *Christian Doctrine of God*, x.

83. Toon, *Doctrine of the Trinity*.

84. Torrance, *Trinitarian Faith*, 127.

85. Basil of Caesarea, *On the Holy Spirit*, 17–18, 48–50.

Development of the Orthodox Doctrine of God's Ontology

only in worship."[86] The liturgical developments demonstrate that deep within the Nicene confession of faith reverberates the cry, "Abba, Father." The truth about the ontological relation of the Father and the Son, while important in and of itself, was also essential to man's salvation because that ontological relation was the basis of a believer's relation to God in the economy of grace. Through anthropocentric reasoning, the soteriological focus that brought subordination to the doctrine of the Trinity actually jeopardized salvation.

CLARITY AT CONSTANTINOPLE

Unfortunately for the faithful, the achievement at Nicaea was not sufficient. Controversy continued, regarding both Christology and soon extending to pneumatology.[87]

Continuing Controversies

Western Arianism of the fourth and fifth centuries was exactly the opposite of Modalism. A more subtle, sophisticated, and dangerous form of the heresy combated at the Council of Nicaea, it sought to separate the Father, the Son, and the Holy Spirit into three separate, distinct beings or essences.[88] It tended toward tritheism in a subordinationism which postulated three gods at three different levels, united in will, purpose, and intent but not in essence or Godhead.[89]

Concerned bishops did not all see eye to eye on the declarations of Nicaea or how the creed itself should be interpreted. Many bishops feared yielding to Modalism[90] as they resisted Arianism.[91] They held that the Son was not inferior to the Father; therefore,

---

86. Studer, *Trinity and Incarnation*, 153.

87. Studer, *Trinity and Incarnation*, 147–48.

88. Torrance, *Trinitarian Faith*, 217.

89. Arius of Alexandria, "Thalia," quoted in Athanasius, "Councils of Ariminum and Seleucia," 458.

90. See glossary for definition.

91. Hägglund, *History of Theology*, 89–91; cf. Calhoun, *Scripture, Creed, Theology*, 247.

he was of like substance (*homoiousios*[92]) with the Father.[93] Such a statement did not keep the Arians out. At times it seemed that the only difference between orthodox *Homoiousions* and Arians was the method they used to weigh the term "like:" either "very like, all but identical"[94] or "slightly resembling."[95]

Philosophy with Humility

Several of the orthodox bishops involved in the great debates labored diligently to close the gap with the *Homoiousions*.[96] Athanasius of Alexandria, for example, urged other bishops to salute them as brothers in the faith because they were clearly not Arians.[97] He admitted that the term *homoiousios* did clearly distinguish the Son from the Father, whereas the term *homoousios* did not.

To overcome this significant difficulty the Cappadocians—Basil of Caesarea, his brother Gregory of Nyssa, and their friend Gregory of Nazianzus—refined the definitions of *ousia* and *hypostasis*.[98] The words *ousia* and *hypostasis*, which at one time had been used as synonyms, had developed deeper meanings through discussion and debate as their original difference was magnified.[99] *Ousia* and *hypostasis* had to have deeper meanings in light of the revelation of God, who is beyond *ousia* and is *ousia* in the strictest sense.[100] *Hypostasis* stressed concrete independence, reality *ad alios* (as opposed to any other). *Ousia* now referred to intrinsic constitution, the reality of a thing that truly resided within that thing.[101]

92. See glossary for definition.
93. Studer, *Trinity and Incarnation*, 109.
94. Torrance, *Trinitarian Faith*, 122–23.
95. Anderson, "Introduction," 8.
96. Studer, *Trinity and Incarnation*, 109–10.
97. Athanasius, "Councils of Ariminum and Seleucia," 472.
98. Studer, *Trinity and Incarnation*, 142–3; see also Calhoun, *Scripture, Creed, Theology*, 249.
99. Toon, *Doctrine of the Trinity*. See also Fortman, *Triune God*, 75–83.
100. Torrance, *Trinitarian Faith*, 79.
101. Torrance, *Trinitarian Faith*, 124–25.

Development of the Orthodox Doctrine of God's Ontology

Thus, in its philosophical application, it [*hypostasis*] could signify either a concrete object or the stuff out of which the concrete object was made. These two nuances closely correspond to the two meanings which Aristotelian philosophy gave to the word *ousia* (οὐσία), which is in derivation the absolute noun corresponding to the verb 'to be.' In Aristotle, the *proto ousia* (or 'first being') is the concrete essence realized in an individual, while the *deutera ousia* ('second being') is the nature which it may share with others of its kind. In Trinitarian theology the former of these usages came to prevail in the case of *hyspostasis* and the latter in the case of *ousia*. Thus the definitive formulation of the doctrine of the Trinity comes to be given in the words, 'three *hypostases* in one *ousia*,' and the Council of Nicaea declared that the Son of God was of the same *ousia* (*homoousios*) with the Father.[102]

Athanasius of Alexandria taught that in God, one and the same substance without change or substitution of content is permanently presented in three distinct and objective forms.[103] God reveals himself through the Son and the Spirit, who inhere in his own eternal being. He thus gives believers such access to himself through Christ and in one Spirit, that they may know God in some measure as he really is in himself in the inner relations of his own triune being.[104] When associated with God's distinct self-revelation in three distinct *hypostaseis*, which are the Father, Son, and Holy Spirit, *ousia* signifies the eternal being, God in the invisible reality and fullness of his intrinsic personal relations as the Holy Trinity.[105] Thus when applied to God, *ousia* had an intensely personal meaning.[106] At last the formula "*mia ousia, treis hypostaseis*" (one essence, three

---

102. Mascall, *Christ, the Christian, and the Church*, 5.
103. Fortman, *Triune God*, 72–79.
104. Studer, *Trinity and Incarnation*, 118.
105. Toon, *Our Triune God*, 41.
106. Torrance, *Christian Doctrine of God*, 119.

persons[107]) gave precise definition to the theology which the ancient church had been struggling for decades to express.[108]

These refined definitions finally gained widespread acceptance at the Council of Constantinople. Slight changes were made there to the Creed of Nicaea in order to both clarify and guard its meaning, forming what is known as the Nicæno-Constantinopolitan Creed (often referred to simply as the Nicene Creed).[109]

The philosophical methods are quite obvious in this development. Greek philosophical ideas "became adapted and transformed in the theological activity of the Church in seeking to understand the nature of God's being, not speculatively from some point outside of God, but from within the actual definitive self-revelation of God in Jesus Christ as Lord and Saviour in the economy of redemption."[110] No slight amount of mental effort went into this conclusion. The orthodox believers, particularly teachers, were loving God with all their mind and strength; they thought carefully and consistently about God's revelation, striving always to hold up Scripture rather than their own interpretation. The result of such humility was charity toward fellow believers, including those of opposing opinions.

> Two years before the Council of Constantinople Epiphanius described the oneness in being between the incarnate Son and the Father, which lay at the heart of the Nicene Creed, as 'the bond of faith' (σύνδεσμος τῆς πίστεως). That is certainly what it has proved to be in the Church: in guiding the faithful in their interpretation of the Holy Scriptures, in clarifying and securing their grasp of evangelical truth, and in enabling them to discern the inner coherent structure of Christian doctrine.[111]

---

107. See glossary.

108. Studer, *Trinity and Incarnation*, 144.

109. The modern debates regarding the magnitude of the changes are beyond the scope of this writing. Nevertheless, no statement of the Creed of Constantinople contradicts or truly alters any statement of the Creed of Nicaea. See also Fortman, *Triune God*, 84–86; Studer, *Trinity and Incarnation*, 159.

110. Torrance, *Christian Doctrine of God*, 117.

111. Torrance, *Trinitarian Faith*, 125.

Development of the Orthodox Doctrine of God's Ontology

CHALCEDON AND BEYOND

Finalizing the Formula

At the Council of Chalcedon, the orthodox doctrine of the Trinity received its final form.[112] Due to the continuing efforts to remain true to the entirety of Scripture, little actual composition was needed at Chalcedon. One might say this council edited the final draft of the creed that was written at Nicaea.[113] Such was, of course, the aim of each successive council—not to improve upon the faith as they had received it, but to preserve that faith.

The Faith of Athanasius

In addition to the conciliar statements, another important creed exists. The exact author is not known; but the creed is formally called the Faith of Athanasius, although it is more commonly known as the Athanasian Creed or the *Quicunque Vult* (after the first two Latin words).[114] The formal title is nevertheless correct since the creed puts forth in concise statement the true doctrine Athanasius taught and worked to establish in the whole church.[115]

In as precise language as is humanly possible, the Athanasian Creed makes an attempt to define the Immanent Trinity, God as he has always been and always will be. Thus the creed sums up the classic Western doctrine of God-as-God-is-in-himself.[116] However, it "does not suggest that 'catholic faith' is merely an intellectual assent but declares, 'now this is the catholic faith that we worship one God in Trinity and Trinity in unity.'"[117] It lists the incommunicable divine attributes by ascribing them one at a time to each of the persons of the Trinity. After describing God's attributes, the Athanasian

---

112. Studer, *Trinity and Incarnation*, 189–90.
113. Calhoun, *Scripture, Creed, Theology*, 308.
114. Fortman, *Triune God*, 158.
115. Torrance, *Christian Doctrine of God*, 96–97.
116. Toon, *Our Triune God*, 232.
117. Fortman, *Triune God*, 160.

Creed proceeds to delineate his eternal position and, subsequently, his eternal interrelations. The relationships of the persons to each other are expressed in scriptural terms.

The creed teaches (as far as spiritually awakened men may perceive) what God is and what he is not. While largely *cataphatic*,[118] the creed, of necessity, inserts an *apophatic*[119] section in order to prevent misinterpretation and heretical teaching. In the first place the creed seeks to detach the discussion of the Trinity from the consideration of the incarnation, resulting in precise understanding of the immanent Trinity.

The doctrine of the incarnation is then fully developed in the second half of the creed. The careful phrasing of this section avoids the christological heresies relating to the humanity of Christ.[120] Taken together the two parts provide an astonishingly balanced approach to how the two views of the Trinity, ontological and economical, work together and complement each other.[121]

As theologians developed more accurate doctrinal formulae, they never lost sight of the truth that God, especially in his nature (though also in his works), is beyond full human comprehension. As Basil Studer concluded,

> In tracing the tenacious struggle for linguistic expression in which the Fathers engaged in order to demarcate the true faith from error, one is not surprised to note that the same Fathers time and again speak with unconcealed reverence of the mysteries of Christian faith, of the divine mysteries. Even in times when precise dogmatic formulation received more authority, a sense was preserved of the ineffability of God and his activity in the world.[122]

Although study and discussion of the nature of the Trinity continued, the widespread acceptance of these creeds brought an end to the serious controversies that had vexed the church for several hundred

---

118. Positive, or asserting what is. See glossary.
119. Negative, or asserting what is not. See glossary.
120. Bishop, *Development of Trinitarian Doctrine*, 4–5.
121. Fortman, *Triune God*, 161.
122. Studer, *Trinity and Incarnation*, 243.

Development of the Orthodox Doctrine of God's Ontology

years. As noted in chapter 1, the Reformed churches accepted all of these creeds as accurate and authoritative in their accordance with Scripture. John Calvin actually contributed to the correct understanding of the Greek concepts of *ousia* and *hypostasis* although he did not use those express words.[123] Only after the Reformation, as the Renaissance was fading in the rise of the Enlightenment, was the orthodox doctrine of the Trinity once more attacked.[124]

---

123. Calvin, *Institutes*, 1.1.13.23. See also Torrance, *Christian Doctrine of God*, 201–2.

124. Toon, *Our Triune God*, 231–32.

Chapter 4

Post-Reformation Rationalism

The Puritan Position

About 1,000 years after the events just related, the same heresies that the councils and creeds had successfully combatted once more reared their ugly heads. The source of these heresies was the same as during the earlier centuries: human reason that forced Scripture into a preconceived philosophical pattern. This time, however, the church as a whole responded quite differently.

By the late 1600s the Protestant Reformation was already history.[1] The works of Luther, Calvin, and other Reformers were now textbooks for serious scholars of theology, rather than "good news from a far country."[2]

Another movement was making an impact on the world. Before the Reformation had drawn fully to a close, the Enlightenment began influencing how Western society viewed the world, themselves, and even the God they worshipped.[3] These two movements,

---

1. Toon, *Emergence of Hyper-Calvinism*, 12.
2. Prov 25:25.
3. Nichols, *History of Christianity*, 94–97.

the Protestant Reformation and the Rationalist Enlightenment, came together to produce an extraordinary offspring: Puritanism.

Puritanism was a subset of Anglicanism which inherited elements both of Lutheran and Reformed theology. The latter was greatly strengthened when, during the reign of "Bloody" Mary, many English Protestants fled to Geneva,[4] while others fled to Holland, another stronghold of Reformed teaching.[5] Returning to England after the accession of Queen Elizabeth I, a number of these exiles manifested new developments in doctrine.[6] Strangely enough, even at this early period just after the death of Calvin,[7] several differences appeared between this reformer's approach to theology and that of his ardent admirers.

NEW VIEWS OF SCRIPTURE

Perhaps the most serious of these differences involved the interpretation of Scripture. The Reformers held a view similar to that held by the ancient councils and the church fathers. As referred to above, in opposition to the Roman Catholic charge that the Reformers were introducing new, strange doctrines, the Reformers stressed their continuity with the teachings of the fathers and their continued commitment to the ecumenical creeds. The church fathers and the creeds served the Reformers much the same as holy tradition and the Rule of Faith had served the ancient fathers.[8] Reformed doctrines were not new; rather, they were merely a return to the true faith of the church.

The Reformers ranked personal reasoning third after Scripture and the ancient doctrinal writings. Their writings soundly evidence that they did indeed employ their reasoning abilities with great diligence. When disagreeing with one of the church fathers, the Reformers took care to respectfully demonstrate how that father had

4. Wallace, "Puritanism, English," 310.
5. Webb, "Emergence of Rational Dissent," 14–16.
6. Wallace, "Puritanism, English," 311.
7. Nichols, *History of Christianity*, 81–82.
8. See chapter 1.

differed from Scripture. *Sola Scriptura* (Scripture alone) for the Reformers signified comparing every teaching, including their own, to God's word. Luther's theology exemplifies this comparison of his own thoughts to Scripture at regular intervals.[9] Calvin also steadily compared Scripture with Scripture to acquire the whole and balanced sense, a practice he respected in others.[10] At the same time, *Solus Christus* (Christ alone) indicated that all revelation from God came through Christ's Spirit. As William Tyndale presented it, the Spirit taught and convinced the believer of true doctrine.[11]

Mechanistic View of Interpretation

Yet as the Reformation progressed (and in many ways came to an end), a subtle shift occurred in the Protestant view of Scripture. Since Holy Scripture was inspired by God, it comprised all truth necessary for salvation, but the focus became the Bible as a collection of true statements instead of the body of revelation continually vitalized by Christ's Spirit.[12] Those who held this view continued to believe that the Spirit's work was necessary for faith, but they did not see Scripture as a book entirely closed to the natural mind.[13] "To say simply that God's ways were beyond human understanding would be to resign from the task, accepted in vigorous good faith and confidence, of making them plain."[14] Soon doctrine was considered to be simply an orderly collection of these true statements from Scripture, and therefore interpretation was held equal with Scripture. All one needed to do is process Scripture logically and the results were guaranteed to be true regardless of one's spiritual state.[15]

The results of this new view were catastrophic. A mechanical view of interpretation led to materialistic, empirical theories about

---

9. Spitz, *Renaissance and Reformation Movements*, 2:347–48.
10. Calvin, *Commentary on a Harmony*, 1:xxxix–xl.
11. Tyndale, "Answer unto Sir Thomas More's Dialogue," 136.
12. Toon, *Emergence of Hyper-Calvinism*, 16–17.
13. May, *Enlightenment in America*, xiv.
14. May, *Enlightenment in America*, 13.
15. Klauber, "Reformed Orthodoxy in Transition," 96–102.

spiritual matters as men replaced the spiritual interpretation with a literal, mechanistic interpretation.[16] "Revelation was information about things of which we would otherwise be ignorant."[17] The Bible was regarded by the orthodox as the revelation of God's nature primarily through his historical acts of redemption.[18] Such a wooden understanding of Scripture soon led to a mechanical view of various doctrines, especially soteriology.

Early Inroads of Rationalism

While the rationalism intrinsic in the mechanical approach to interpretation is obvious, where did it come from? During this time various philosophies had developed regarding the thinking process. One of the earliest of these philosophies and the one which would have the greatest impact on Puritanism was developed by Frenchman Peter Ramus.[19] His system of organizing all truths into dichotomies fascinated Englishmen, Puritans in particular.[20] Since Ramist philosophy presupposed that all truths were the same as facts and that all facts could be employed like blocks of knowledge,[21] the Puritan interpretation of Scripture soon reflected a wooden, dichotomistic approach. The impacts of such an approach on the doctrines of the incarnation and the Holy Trinity did not appear until later after they had become grave dangers.[22]

Other philosophies of reasoning also affected Puritanism and the Reformed churches in general. Nevertheless, whether the false dichotomies of Ramist thinking, the subtle but perverse material

---

16. Nichols, *History of Christianity*, 97–98.
17. Nichols, *History of Christianity*, 100.
18. Webb, "Emergence of Rational Dissent," 19.
19. Hannah, "Sources of American Puritan Theology," Chart 63.
20. Toon, *Emergence of Hyper-Calvinism*, 24–25; McKim, "Ramus, Peter (1515–1572)," 314.
21. Foxgrover, "Self-Examination in John Calvin and William Ames," 452, 460.
22. Webb, "Emergence of Rational Dissent," 7.

empiricism of Scottish Common Sense and John Locke,[23] or the skepticism of Descartes,[24] all Enlightenment philosophies shared the basic assumption that man could and must grasp truth by his own reasoning ability. Man's reason in its natural state possessed the power to give judgment on all that man might encounter[25] and was the glorious part of human nature that enabled man to rule himself and all creation, as well as to interact with God.[26] While firmly holding to the doctrine of original sin, Puritans came to believe that Scripture and nature appealed to man's mind to convince him morally and ethically of God's existence and the honor and service due him. As leading Puritan William Perkins wrote, "It is also requisite that this doctrine [of God] agree with the grounds of common reason, and of that knowledge of God which may be obtained by the light of nature."[27] Such natural light cast an inverted upward shadow.

EMPHASIS ON THE WORKS OF GOD OVER HIS NATURE

Emphasis on Soteriology

A great deal has been written to discuss and debate the place of rationalism and emotionalism in Puritan theology. Were Puritans primarily rational or emotional? The answer is yes since the Puritans were both highly rational and almost equally emotional.[28] Many of them abandoned resting in Christ and began working earnestly for Christ out of gratitude for all he had undertaken. Realizing that more often than not they served God for his spiritual benefits instead of serving him out of unselfish devotion and that their best repentance needed to be repented of, the Puritans began

23. May, *Enlightenment in America*, 5–10.
24. Descartes, "Certainty of Self and God" 111–12, 116.
25. Nichols, *History of Christianity*, 94.
26. May, *Enlightenment in America*, 10.
27. Perkins, "Letter No. 9, Epistle to the Reader," 291.
28. Wallace, "Puritanism, English," 311.

Post-Reformation Rationalism

to psychologically implode.[29] Only proper devotion was befitting to effectual grace. The categories of duty and grace did not allow for any other possibility.

Actually the conundrum was produced by rationalism. Salvation was divided between God's work and its results.[30] God made certain demands of man. Without Christ it was impossible to fulfill those demands; with Christ it was expected that a person would be living in accordance with the demands of a holy God.[31] As a result Puritanism eventually became divided. Although the emotionalism and rationalism both had their source in will power,[32] they could not continue to coexist indefinitely as equals. In spite of the two major trends in Puritanism, not every Puritan fell into the ditch or into the mire.[33] For those who realized the full implications of salvation (that they were indeed the objects of triune love with everlasting life springing within them from no efforts of their own) thorough meditation on Christ produced some of the deepest devotional literature since Bernard of Clairvaux.[34]

That soteriology received the greatest emphasis can easily be seen from the foregoing summary of Puritanism. The chief question was "Am I truly converted?" "One of the chief characteristics of Puritanism was its great interest in the doctrine of the assurance of eternal salvation.... The Puritans concerned themselves with what they considered to be the most important question of all."[35] Among other reasons, including the theological instability of the times, these people thought this question "useful and practical."[36] Notice: they did not ask what one must do to be saved but rather how does one know with certainty that he is saved.[37] Many wor-

---

29. Lim, *Mystery Unveiled*, 193.
30. Foxgrover, "Self-Examination in John Calvin and William Ames," 463.
31. Webb, "Emergence of Rational Dissent," 17.
32. Benjamin, *Simply Singular*, 22.
33. Bunyan, *Pilgrim's Progress*, 66.
34. Wallace, "Puritanism, English," 311.
35. Toon, *Emergence of Hyper-Calvinism*, 17.
36. Toon, *Emergence of Hyper-Calvinism*, 17.
37. Wallace, "Puritanism, English," 311.

ried that they might not be one of the elect. In vain did Calvin and others after him insist that election was none of man's business; he was only required to believe on the Lord Jesus Christ.

> Many persons, as soon as they learn that none are heirs of eternal life but those whom God *chose before the foundation of the world*, (Eph. i.4,) begin to inquire anxiously how they may be assured of God's secret purpose, and thus plunge into a labyrinth, from which they will find no escape. Christ enjoins them to come direct to himself, in order to obtain certainty of salvation. The meaning therefore is, that life is exhibited to us in Christ himself, and that no man will partake of it who does not enter by the gate of faith. We now see that he connects faith with the eternal predestination of God,—two things which men foolishly and wickedly hold to be inconsistent with each other. Though our salvation was always hidden with God, yet Christ is the channel through which it flows to us, and we receive it by faith, that it may be secure and ratified in our hearts.[38]

But these were enlightened times. Therefore all that occurred or could be thought of was man's business, and from the Puritan point of view, a man's soul ought to be his greatest business; and thus the thinking went in a circle, as rationalistic thought usually does.

The Puritan obsession with one's own salvation and holiness was due in part to a change of focus. Instead of seeking to know the Father in Christ by the Spirit through the written word, the Puritans sought to correctly assemble the truths concerning God and humanity from the collection of Holy Scriptures. The increased sense of reason's ability also led to an unbearable sense of responsibility to act in keeping with the light provided in nature and Scripture. For example, William Perkins taught that believers can use good works to assure themselves of salvation, as opposed to Calvin's emphasis "on personal faith in Christ and union to Him as well as on God's sanctifying gifts to His people."[39]

---

38. Calvin, *Commentary on a Harmony*, 2:40; italics original.
39. Toon, *Emergence of Hyper-Calvinism*, 17.

Post-Reformation Rationalism

Misunderstanding Divine Sovereignty

The emphasis on soteriology, coupled with the mechanical view of Scripture, resulted in the development of misunderstandings concerning divine sovereignty. God was not viewed as sovereign over himself as a free agent but more like a mechanical force that operated according to its properties or, worse, as part of a great chain of cause and effect. Depending on the conditions met, God had to punish or forgive. The moral law was viewed by some as independently obligatory to God himself rather than a reflection of his nature.[40]

The last representation was not common until the thorough spread of natural theology; nevertheless for many theologians, regardless of how highly conservative they were, the concept of God's free will somehow became separated from his gracious salvation. For all intents and purposes, God's will became attributed solely to his electing decrees or other eternal decrees.[41] Redemption was divided into election and the *missio Dei*,[42] the sending of the Son and the Spirit into the world. Since these two were always discussed separately, they seem to have become compartmentalized. Although orthodox men declared free grace as the source of the *missio Dei*, the course of covenant-making in eternity past ran mechanistically on its own after divine goodness had started it on its way. Furthermore, many of Calvin's followers ignored his warnings against speculation into the decrees of election and reprobation. They then assigned chronological order to God's eternal decrees.[43] This view would have profound impacts on the doctrine of the Trinity.

---

40. May, *Enlightenment in America*, 12; see also Miller, "Marrow of Puritan Divinity," 16–17.

41. Perkins, "Letter No. 9, Epistle to the Reader," 291–92.

42. See glossary for definition.

43. Toon, *Emergence of Hyper-Calvinism*, 13–14.

Definition of Hyper-Calvinism

Before looking at those impacts, one ought to pause and observe how far Reformed theology had departed from the teaching of the Reformers. Calvin had stressed the love of God and his continual intervening grace in the affairs of men.[44] Believers ought to follow Christ faithfully; however, for Calvin the Triune God did the work of salvation and sanctification in his children in order that they could learn to rest in his nature.[45] The focus was on God who provided salvation, rather than on the salvation God provided. Such a small difference of beginning produced a vastly different end result.

In many ways Puritanism, with its emphasis on the divine decrees instead of on the divine essence and on personal salvation and sanctification rather than on the love of God, was as a theological system hyper-Calvinist.[46] Linking hyper-Calvinism with an overemphasis on soteriology may seem extraordinary to many, but in truth such an overemphasis is the very origin of hyper-Calvinism.

A warning is in order. Various people define hyper-Calvinism differently. The result is often little more than quibbling. Many use the test of "free offer" of the gospel to distinguish a hyper-Calvinist from a Calvinist. While this test offers a starting point, it is not sufficiently comprehensive and overlooks theological matters of much greater weight, such as the nature of the God who saves and the nature of the soteriology which developed. Both sides of the "free offer" debate seem to have become consumed with soteriological questions to the sad and dangerous neglect of the One "from whom all blessings flow." Both sides have become anthropocentric in their reasoning about the gospel and perhaps blinded to a slow slip both in the view of God's sovereignty as stemming from his nature, as well as the true nature of the Trinity.

A more objective definition of hyper-Calvinism is offered by the Shorter Oxford English Dictionary: "A hyper-Calvinist is a person who holds a doctrine (especially of predestination) more

---

44. See especially Calvin's *Commentaries on the Book of Joshua*.
45. Calvin, *Institutes*, 1.3.3.9.
46. Toon, *Emergence of Hyper-Calvinism*, 143–44.

Calvinistic than Calvin's own."[47] Peter Toon demonstrates the quality of this definition in *The Emergence of Hyper-Calvinism in English Non-Conformity*. Starting with Calvin's teaching, he discusses each major English Reformed group together with the changes that developed in their doctrine and compares each with Calvin's teaching.

A second warning is that hyper-Calvinism lies directly on the frontier of Arminianism. This will become more evident in the examination of Charles Chauncy. Any shift of focus off of God as Trinity may result in some form of Arminianism. This is not to say that all hyper-Calvinists are really Arminian, but rather the danger for hyper-Calvinism is as great as that posed by Arminianism.

Nevertheless, hyper-Calvinism is not like mold on pudding: it does not necessarily contaminate all of a person's doctrine. Being a hyper-Calvinist does not mean a person can never make a positive contribution to the life of the church in his own day and beyond.

EVENTUAL STRONG SUBORDINATIONISM IN THE DOCTRINE OF THE TRINITY

The shift from Calvin's focus on the love of God to the emphasis on soteriology with its concomitant misunderstandings of sovereignty eventually resulted as a matter of course in an establishment of the economic view of the Trinity as equal or superior to the ontological view. Obviously if one's salvation is that which he should most concern himself about, then what God did and does for man's salvation should be primary in one's thought.[48] Naturally, this much focus on what God did resulted in some loss of understanding of the nature of the God who did this work. The relationship between the persons of the Godhead in eternity were defined by their interaction in time.

---

47. "Hyper-Calvinism," *Shorter Oxford English Dictionary (OED)*.
48. Lim, *Mystery Unveiled*, 179.

The Economic Trinity Equal or Superior to the Ontological Trinity

The dreadful result of this redefinition was subordinationism. The humiliation of Christ and his submission to the Father were read back into the precreation councils of the Trinity. In the Puritans' doctrine of Federal Theology,[49] the covenant of grace was usually taught thus: The Father dictated the conditions of redemption to the Son. The Son humbly accepted the conditions the Father demanded while the Spirit stood by and witnessed the transaction.[50] In this interpretation of the eternal councils, the Son and the Spirit are not co-equal with the Father. Instead, the Son is inferior to the Father, and the Spirit is inferior to the Son.[51] This is a form of the semi-Arianism Athanasius worked earnestly to overcome.[52] As a result, the attitude of the Father toward men was misunderstood. The Father became almost as unapproachable as Arius had pictured him. All was left up to the Son.

The implications of Puritan theology were largely unrecognized by those who held this position.[53] When in the last part of the eighteenth century men began to openly espouse these latent errors, orthodox Puritans resisted such teaching as heterodox at best. Nevertheless, these implications permitted Puritans to be powerfully influenced by the rationalist redefinition of the doctrine of the Trinity, especially as systematized by Samuel Clarke.[54]

---

49. Note: the Puritan doctrine described here is not definitive for Federal Theology as a whole. See glossary for definition of basic Federal Theology.

50. Toon, *Emergence of Hyper-Calvinism*, 112–14.

51. See the movement of divine communication between the persons of the Godhead in Perkins's "Chart of Salvation and Damnation," 295–300.

52. Kelly, *Early Christian Doctrines*, 249–51.

53. Lim, *Mystery Unveiled*, 183–87.

54. Webb, "Emergence of Rational Dissent," 26–27.

Post-Reformation Rationalism

The Covenant Inverted and Reversed

Such a view of the work of the Trinity in redemption misconstrues the economy of grace, picturing the covenant of grace[55] inverted and reversed. The covenant is inverted because it exists primarily for man's good (salvation) rather than God's glory. Man's redemption ought rather to be understood as based in the glory of God, not in man's need anymore than his merit.[56] Such an understanding is both required by Scripture and is also the only solid foundation for soteriology. God saves for his name's sake,[57] for his mercy's sake, not for anything desirable in the one saved. God then creates what is lacking in his own purchased possession.[58] Salvation grounded in the nature and glory of God is a sure salvation indeed. The covenant thus pictured is also reversed because it projects time back into eternity past by treating the conditions of redemption as synonymous with conditions of the incarnation and by assigning a chronological order to God's eternal decrees, a mistake Calvin expressly warned against.[59]

As persons of the Trinity, Christ and the Spirit ought to be understood as originators of the redemption plan alongside the Father. The truth is that a covenant is an extended form of a promise.[60] The covenant is in Christ because he made it, not as a pact with the Father on man's behalf, but as a promise, a creation.

The Puritans were certainly not alone in holding to Federal Theology, nor did they typically take it to its extreme logical end. The original teaching of Federal Theology (which several Reformed groups continue to teach) does have certain trinitarian weaknesses in relation to the covenant of redemption. However the Puritans modified this doctrine slightly by including what they considered its logical inferences, inferences that other Reformed groups did not always accept (an example of hyper-Calvinism).

55. Also known as the covenant of redemption.
56. Ps 79:9; Isa 48:9–11; Jer 14:21.
57. Ps 25:11; Ezek 36:22; 1 John 2:12.
58. Calvin, *Bondage and Liberation of the Will*, 136.
59. Calvin, *Concerning the Eternal Predestination of God*, 125.
60. OED.

> Into that [Reformed] tradition, under the guise of a doctrine of covenants made by God with man there had been injected many ideas which derived, not from theology and revelation, but from law, from the study of nature, from the principles of reason and common sense. As time went on, the incompatibility of these ideas with the official confession was bound to become more apparent.[61]

Yet this modified version of Federal Theology had a widespread and lasting impact on evangelicalism as a whole. Additionally, Puritans held Federal Theology more centrally and with greater logical stricture than others with the same doctrine. In many ways this combination of moderation and rigid application of philosophy in theology exemplifies the conservative evangelical position from their day until now.

---

61. Miller, "Marrow of Puritan Divinity," 42.

Chapter 5

Charles Chauncy and the Liberal Position

Effects of the Enlightenment

SPIRITUAL AND PHILOSOPHICAL BACKGROUNDS OF CHARLES CHAUNCY AND JOHN GILL

Out of this spiritual and philosophical background arose Charles Chauncy and John Gill. Although both Charles Chauncy and John Gill spiritually descend from British Puritanism, they received that tradition in various forms. American and British Puritanism had begun going their separate ways long before Charles Chauncy or John Gill ministered.[1] That both strains of Puritanism continued to emphasize the rational part of theology shows how intrinsic this rational theology was to Puritanism.

In some ways American Puritanism (which became known as Congregationalism) was in a worse spiritual condition than its British counterpart; in other ways the reverse was true. Mediocrity remained the chief fault of American Puritanism with the

---

1. Walker, *The Creeds and Platforms of Congregationalism*, 134–43. See also Guelzo, "Puritanism, American," 308.

no-more-desirable counterpart of emotionalism. In Britain, stark heresies were flagrantly accepted by some in the church. This had the positive effect of drawing the orthodox more closely together. However, the most serious threat came in the form of debates with those promoting error. Since Puritanism and its descendants stood on the insecure footing of Scripture mixed with rationalism, their opponents could easily force them into an unbalanced or untenable position.

Separated from their English brethren, American Puritanism began to slowly shift.[2] Theirs were not the dramatic divisions such as rent England. In some ways orthodoxy held out longer in New England; in other ways it slid more easily. Many are the scholars who have studied this paradoxical character of New England Puritanism. Suffice it to say Americans have always been Americans since they were first born on the shores of that continent;[3] and the world may take a warning, the Americans most of all.

CHARLES CHAUNCY (1705-1787)

His Life and Controversies

Charles Chauncy was born in New England to a distinguished Congregationalist family. The young Charles Chauncy received a quality Puritan education, first at home and then as a student at Harvard University. Soon after finishing his education, Chauncy was ordained and became the colleague pastor of First Church, Boston, and eventually became the senior pastor upon the death of Thomas Foxcroft in 1769.

During Chauncy's long ministry at First Church, he became the leading pastor of Boston,[4] and in many ways of all New England. He would always be remembered as a pastor and as a scholar. Both Charles Lippy and Edward Griffin[5] ably demonstrate how Chauncy

---

2. James, *New England Puritans*, 12.
3. Lippy, *Seasonable Revolutionary*, 19-23.
4. Walker, *Ten New England Leaders*, 299.
5. Griffin, *Old Brick*.

Charles Chauncy and the Liberal Position

strove to preserve the Puritan doctrines he had received, while at the same time considering and finally embracing the most radical natural theology of his day. The New England version of Puritanism that Chauncy inherited had already manifested a strong affinity with the heavy rational emphasis and effort-driven sanctification of William Perkins, William Ames, and Richard Baxter.[6] As Lippy and Griffin point out, although Chauncy's mature writings shocked many New England Puritans, his thought moved in a direct line from older Puritan theology.

"Many conflicts were to be a part of his life as the older Puritanism faded into the newer rationalism. Chauncy's life bridges the gap between these two ways of life. . . . The views which Chauncy adopted during this period were to have increased importance during the years following his death."[7] Two controversies in particular sharpened Charles Chauncy's theological definitions and made his opinions widely public. The first and primary controversy was the Great Awakening.

One of the many effects the Great Awakening had on Puritanism was the magnification of both the rationalism and the emotionalism inherent within it. The Great Awakening represented Puritanism coming apart at the seams. For some, the emotional experience was the confirmation of election they desperately craved.[8] How could they be assured their evidences of grace were true tokens of conversion? Here was a definite event they could point to and say, "There, now I know I have the seal of the Spirit." For others, diligent attendance on the means of grace and lives conforming to the moral law became satisfactory indications that one was in good standing before God.[9] A checklist had to be sufficient. They could not keep up the agonizing.[10]

From Chauncy's perspective the excesses of the awakening were not merely incidental to a few fanatics, but revealed essential

---

6. Hannah, "Sources of American Puritan Theology," Chart 63.
7. Linden, "Charles Chauncy," i.
8. Maclear, "'Heart of New England Rent,'" 45.
9. Miller, "Marrow of Puritan Divinity," 26.
10. See Stout, *New England Soul*, 35–38, for a description from primary sources of this agonizing.

flaws in the theology that supported the awakening itself.[11] Chauncy believed that a man's reason must absolutely control his religion. Emotion must remain in its proper, secondary place. However, the central questions of the awakening did not simply concern a philosophical evaluation of the relation of reason to emotion in human psychology. The debates centered on the place of pneumatology in soteriology and how the assurance of salvation is obtained.[12]

From historians Charles Chauncy has received attention primarily as the "liberal" opponent to Jonathan Edwards during the Great Awakening. On the contrary, Charles Chauncy did not merely side with the rational over emotional aspect of the fracturing Puritan tradition; he took the problematic aspects of Puritanism to their logical end.[13] This is why he never fully departed from Puritan doctrine, although by the end of his life his writings consternated Calvinists.

A second controversy evidenced more clearly Chauncy's modifications of Puritan teaching. A minor agitation developed in the greater Boston area over the publication of a small treatise known as "A Summer-Morning's Conversation, concerning Original Sin" by Peter Clark.[14] In it the author attempted to defend a drastically hyper-Calvinistic position on predestination, including that of infants. The publication of this treatise brought into the open a developing schism in New England Congregationalism. Many New England pastors, influenced by the books on natural theology that had been coming over from England, had begun to entertain doubts about the doctrine of election.[15] Charles Chauncy numbered among them, and several of his acquaintances looked to him to answer Peter Clark. However, the books on natural theology that Chauncy had read affected not only his doctrine of election but also his entire doctrinal system. The answer Chauncy composed to "A Summer-Morning's Conversation" evidenced this change less

11. Lippy, *Seasonable Revolutionary*, 27.
12. Maclear, "'Heart of New England Rent,'" 48.
13. Walker, *Ten New England Leaders*, 297.
14. Clark, "Scripture-Doctrine of Original Sin."
15. Walker, *Ten New England Leaders*, 274, 297–98.

subtly than his previous publications,[16] causing the first real stir of concern among those who read his sermons and writings.

Chauncy's writings display a fairly gradual development in his theological opinions. Notwithstanding, he spent an extended period of time studying Scripture in light of the new books on natural theology and the text-critical method.[17] Unfortunately, his early theological training ill-prepared him to evaluate whether Scripture should be thus understood or to measure the new theology by Scripture instead of vice versa. Soon his theological shadows were stretching upward.

His Mature Teachings on God's Ontology

The purpose here is not to explore the development of Charles Chauncy's theology, but to examine his mature writings and evaluate their theological statements. The best source on Chauncy's view of God's ontology is his book *Benevolence of the Deity*. The purpose of the book is to demonstrate that the attribute of benevolence is the basic essence of God making all his other attributes worthy of being called divine.[18] This benevolence is understood by man's intuition (which Chauncy labeled reason), by the laws of creation in their original intention, and, in part, by the visible world. God is primarily benevolent; all else is secondary and derived. God's benevolence caused him to create all things and to allow them to be the way they are.

God is transcendent, but not wholly other. God's nature is different from man's nature in amount of any attribute considered, but not in kind. God is superior to man in much the same manner an adult is superior to a child. Chauncy denies that God's moral character differs from man's moral character in aught but magnitude.[19] God is primarily Creator and Sustainer (Providence), secondarily

16. Chauncy, "Opinion of One."
17. Walker, *Ten New England Leaders*, 200–301.
18. Chauncy, *Benevolence*, iv–v.
19. Chauncy, *Benevolence*, 14–18.

Redeemer. More accurately, God makes salvation possible for anyone that desires it.[20]

According to Charles Chauncy, the divine being finds himself constrained to work within self-existent absolutes, both moral and physical (a type of pagan Platonism). That which is right is right; and since God as God only does what is right, he had to follow the order of what man commonly understands as right. Objects in creation, whether round or square, had to be created in accord with round or square properties.[21] Only what is consistent with common human experience (as Chauncy knows it) is real,[22] although the commonality of human experience that provides the basis for Chauncy's arguments is often restricted to educated persons. The masses do not exercise their reason sufficiently to possess a meaningful experience. The educated man observes the laws of nature, consults his own conscience, and deduces truth about right and wrong along with an understanding of how creation was originally intended to be. From these propositions man discovers the truth about God's nature and his attitude toward mankind.

Chauncy does not disregard Scripture entirely. While viewing it as necessary for knowledge of God, Chauncy nevertheless believed that the meaning of Scripture must be understood from the viewpoint of human experience. For example, since Chauncy did not know of anyone who felt guilt for original sin, Scripture could not be interpreted as teaching the death of every person in Adam.

Sin and death (griefs that are the sources of all other griefs that exist) are a necessary part of the world.[23] Natural disasters, death, and such like are simply part of the way God had to create the world in order that the system of creation would be best overall. God was bound by necessity. However, he could not bind man necessarily to heaven or hell[24] although man had to endure the griefs and difficulties of this life that God, most loving and gracious, could not have

20. Miller, "Marrow of Puritan Divinity," 21.

21. Chauncy, *Benevolence*, 33–37.

22. Chauncy, *Benevolence*, 136–37. Nichols urges that this is standard Enlightenment thought (*History of Christianity*, 95–97).

23. Chauncy, *Benevolence*, 255–73.

24. Chauncy, *Benevolence*, viii, 128–36.

Charles Chauncy and the Liberal Position

prevented if he was to do his best by all of his creation. "It may be said, the bringing into existence an absolutely perfect creature is not within the reach of infinite goodness, aided by almighty power."[25] Every man is the product of his parents[26] and endowed with a certain amount of mental ability, which he then is responsible to improve. Some will advance further than others from the start they receive. Those with setbacks, such as bad genes or an unfavorable upbringing, who improve themselves morally, will receive a better reward in the next life.[27] Griefs from other people's sins build character and offer opportunity to exercise greater moral goodness.

Application to the Doctrine of the Trinity

From this summary one can perceive that God achieved the best he could in creating the world and now sits by with only enough input to keep things functioning. Part of that input, however, included having Jesus Christ come to earth.[28] In *The Mystery Hid* (also known as *The Salvation of All*) Chauncy makes his clearest statements of his Christology. Christ's life on earth during his incarnation was of paramount importance. Jesus provided the model upon which all people were to pattern their lives. An upright life, lived in obedience to the moral law and accompanied by prayer and diligent religious observation, made one acceptable to God.

Conformity to God's moral law was highly important to the Puritans.[29] As Puritanism began emphasizing the works of God rather than his nature, the same inevitably became the focus of believers concerning their own works versus their nature. The work of God in them, having been confused with their works as its manifestations, became paramount to the neglect of the new

---

25. Chauncy, *Benevolence*, 183.
26. Chauncy, *Benevolence*, 274–67
27. Chauncy, *Benevolence*, 249.
28. Chauncy, *Benevolence*, 166–7, 172–73; also, Chauncy, *Mystery Hid*, 1–3, 12–15.
29. Ahlstrom, *Religious History of the American People*, 153.

nature, Christ's life in them.[30] The emphasis on a believer's works resulted in Neo-nomianism: the gospel began to be treated as a new law.[31] One writer who was largely responsible for introducing Neo-nomianism into Puritanism was Richard Baxter,[32] who had a great impact on Chauncy.[33]

Charles Chauncy took Neo-nomianism to its logical end: if one can be pleasing to God only if he keeps the commandments, then he must simply focus on keeping the commandments; and he will necessarily be pleasing to God as long as he continues to employ the New Testament institutions accordingly. Faith was not eliminated but became relegated to a secondary place.[34]

What of a person's sins? Christ's death was satisfactory before God to atone for the sin of anyone who applied for that atonement.[35] True, no one would have acceptance before God without the atonement in Christ, but God was obligated to tender it to anyone who asked.[36]

In discussing the incarnation, Charles Chauncy's Christology carries a highly kenotic flavor. Chauncy emphasized the humanity and humiliation of Christ to the point of implicitly denying his deity. In reference to Colossians 2:9, Chauncy wrote:

> By this *fullness of the Godhead* we are to understand, not that *absolute fullness of all perfection* which belongs to the *Deity*, but that *fullness of gifts and grace*, which the Godhead intends *by him* to impart to *others*. . . . The meaning is, that he is *really* and *truly* possessed . . . of *all the transient fullness of God*, or, as the same may be expressed in other words, that he is the glorious *person in which* God has *really* lodged, and *through whom* he will actually communicate *all that fullness* wherewith he

---

30. Miller, "Marrow of Puritan Divinity," 16.
31. Chauncy, "Ministers Exhorted," 14–15.
32. Toon, *Emergence of Hyper-Calvinism*, 23.
33. Griffin, *Old Brick*, 109.
34. Chauncy, "Minsters Exhorted," 17.
35. Chauncy, *Mystery Hid*, 19–22.
36. Miller, "Marrow of Puritan Divinity," 25.

Charles Chauncy and the Liberal Position

intends this *lapsed world* shall be *filled*, in order to its restoration.[37]

The result becomes some form of adoptionist Christology, a form of Arianism.[38] Nor does it end there because Chauncy minimized the deity and maximized the humanity of Christ to the point of subordinationism even after Christ's exultation.

The Holy Spirit was the gift of God bestowed on those who, attending faithfully on the means of grace, fulfilled all the conditions. In addition to bestowing God's grace on an individual, the Spirit strove to persuade a person of the truth and the need of religion.

When applied to the doctrine of the Holy Trinity, the result of Charles Chauncy's teaching was distinct subordinationism. In some regards he viewed the Spirit as more divine than Christ. Obviously, the relations of the persons of the Godhead, if indeed the Son and the Spirit were considered such, had their foundation of definition in man's salvation. The subordinationism intrinsic to the hyper-Calvinist view of the covenant of redemption came into sharp focus. The benevolent Father had arranged for the salvation of men by sending Christ to earth.

The question remained as to who Christ was essentially. While entitling Jesus "Son of God," Chauncy nevertheless focused heavily on Christ as Mediator and Example.[39] "Chauncy was a high Arian. Christ was to him an object of worship; faith in Christ was the condition of our salvation. Our acceptance with God is founded on the 'blood and righteousness' of Christ. Christ is the 'all in all,' the sovereign of this dispensation; yet he is not God, nor equal with God."[40] In fact, the most important aspect of Christ's death was his obedient submission to the Father, for which the Father greatly rewarded him.[41] Christ's obedience to the Father continues as he serves as

---

37. Chauncy, *Mystery Hid*, 124; italics original.

38. See Kelly, *Early Christian Doctrines*, 132–36.

39. Lippy, *Seasonable Revolutionary*, 117; see also Nichols, *History of Christianity*, 96–97.

40. Walker, *Ten New England Leaders*, 308.

41. Walker, *Ten New England Leaders*, 186.

Mediator for man.[42] In the end, Christ would yield the kingdom he had received from the Father at his exaltation back to the Father, to whom he would then be forever subject.[43] Chauncy never seemed to understand what a disgusting end would result from this approach to Christ's crucifixion.[44] Chauncy continued to firmly believe in the necessity of the blood of Christ to atone for man's sin. However, the Puritan obsession with election (especially assurance) and preparation for grace had already obscured the complete sufficiency of Christ's sacrifice as it was applied by the grace of the Spirit through faith to the soul.[45] Therefore for Chauncy, Christ "demonstrated that attainment of ultimate happiness was a real possibility for ordinary human beings. Equally important, Christ served as an example of the life which persons intent on eternal happiness should lead."[46]

Man's entire moral independence of God is necessary to true happiness because being confident that one did right by his own choice provides the greatest happiness. God desires above all else that man be happy; therefore, God will not interfere with anything that will cause those comfortable feelings of happiness. Consequently, God forgives man through Christ, but will not assist anyone morally or otherwise infringe on a person's choices.[47] Self-assurance is the greatest pleasure or happiness in this life and the best brace against death.

"Puritans had long spoken of divine sovereignty; Charles Chauncy simply claimed that divine benevolence presented itself as the best manifestation of that sovereignty."[48] Once again the result was not what any early Puritan would have recognized as sovereignty. According to Chauncy, God's benevolence requires the happiness of his creatures. Evil in the world must be inevitable

---

42. Walker, *Ten New England Leaders*, 14–15.
43. Chauncy, *Mystery Hid*, 147–49.
44. Mascall, *Christ, the Christian, and the Church*, 75, 88.
45. Miller, "Marrow of Puritan Divinity," 29.
46. Lippy, *Seasonable Revolutionary*, 118.
47. Chauncy, *Benevolence*, 218–21.
48. Lippy, *Seasonable Revolutionary*, 122.

because no finer system of creation could have been possible.[49] God as good in himself would have contradicted his nature if he had not made creation as good as it could be. Though man may not be able to comprehend how evil could be best in the end, nevertheless he must trust God's wisdom and goodness.[50] Not all evil was incomprehensible, however: some of it could be explained by the application of good reason.

Application to Sovereignty Resulting in Universalism

"Free will was an almost universal dogma of the Enlightenment religion, and in order to assert it the doctrines of depravity and predestination were almost universally rejected."[51] For man to be truly happy, according to Charles Chauncy, he must have the ability, among others, to be self-determining.[52] The result of this self-determination in Adam had been the fall, not from a world of physical perfection but his own moral perfection. Consequently human nature is not sinful *per se*, but fundamentally flawed; and for that reason any man born naturally will eventually sin, becoming at that moment a sinner. In the end, therefore, all men are sinners and in need of a Savior. As pointed out before, God, in his benevolence, provided for the salvation of mankind in Christ.[53]

The problem still continued to exist: What if a self-determined man chose to refuse God's great kindness extended in Christ? Not only would evil remain that would necessitate some sort of action on God's part, but Charles Chauncy also faced the difficulties that Calvinists of his era had pointed out to the Arminians. If Christ died for all mankind and some people, many in fact, refused to accept his sacrifice on their behalf, then to whatever degree Christ's sacrifice was neglected or refused, it was in vain.[54]

---

49. Chauncy, *Benevolence*, 67, 74.
50. Chauncy, *Benevolence*, 178.
51. Nichols, *History of Christianity*, 96.
52. Chauncy, *Benevolence*, 49.
53. Chauncy, *Twelve Sermons*, 156.
54. Cf. Gill, *Cause of God and Truth*, 3.3.2, with Chauncy, *Mystery Hid*, 22.

Since the idea of Christ's gracious sacrifice and God's extended kindness being in vain was foreign to the excellencies of God and his promises (not to mention his care even for those rebels), Charles Chauncy concluded that all men must eventually be saved.[55] God knew that if evil remained unpunished, it would certainly ruin his creation. Yet if he punished evil men eternally, those souls would not be happy; and God would seem harsh and cruel.[56] Although Chauncy thought God's benevolence was the source of happiness to his creation in this life, true happiness consisted in the ultimate sanctification and fulfillment of the soul in the life to come. Indeed, those whose only happiness in this life was the self-assurance that they were doing right would be all the more rewarded in the next life and there find greater happiness than those who had been fortunate on earth.[57]

Therefore for God to be true to his benevolent nature and fulfill his promises as Charles Chauncy interpreted them, he must provide means for even evil men to be saved in the end. What may seem like a long and largely unsupported chain of logic was in fact indispensable to Chauncy's theology. "Once Chauncy insisted on the paramount position of benevolence among God's attributes, he had to face the doctrinal consequences."[58] If his system contained one error, it promised ruin to the system in its entirety and would perhaps even bring eternal loss. It would most certainly indicate that Chauncy had not used his reason correctly.

Soteriological Focus

Charles Chauncy inherited an advanced form of American Puritanism that was already experiencing the effects of the early Enlightenment. The covenant idea of Puritanism was not quite in keeping with the rest of covenantal theology as taught by the Reformed

---

55. Chauncy, *Mystery Hid*, 1–3, 22.
56. Chauncy, *Mystery Hid*, 9–12.
57. Chauncy, *Benevolence*, 248–9.
58. Griffin, *Old Brick*, 112.

churches[59] because it incorporated a conversion experience as well as acceptance into the church based on the relation of a qualifying conversion testimony. The Half-Way Covenant of 1662 went far toward reducing emphasis on experience and magnifying the effects of church membership in spiritual development.[60] Perhaps key to the shift of doctrine in New England was the teaching of preparation for grace, a matter upon which head Puritans were by no means agreed. Still, some of the "great founding fathers of the New England Way... each in his own way, developed elaborate doctrines of preparation for grace until the process came to be regarded as an essential stage in the order of salvation."[61] Nevertheless for many, focus had shifted from Christ to the sacraments. Not that the sacraments were believed to have independent power, but they were the primary means of grace.[62] Other means of grace included prayer and the word, read and preached. Unlike other groups who knew and used the means of grace as believers, the New England Puritans used them as preparation for grace.[63] No one knows whether he is elect and thus will be saved; but in hopes that he might be, he ought to try to prepare himself for the coming of special grace. In that way lay the only direction from which the Spirit would come.[64]

Repeatedly, almost monotonously, Charles Chauncy proclaimed the means of grace as the road to salvation.

> We can no more be made righteous by the righteousness of another transferred to us, and reckoned our's, than we can be made sinners by the sin of another transferred in like manner. They are both moral impossibilities, and equally so.
>
> That part therefore of the advantage through Christ, which consists in our being made righteous, and in this

---

59. See Miller, "Marrow of Puritan Divinity," for an extensive explanation and discussion of this change.

60. Lippy, *Seasonable Revolutionary*, 30.

61. Ahlstrom, *Religious History*, 152.

62. Chauncy, "Only Compulsion Proper," 20.

63. Miller, "Marrow of Puritan Divinity," 31.

64. Stout, *New England Soul*, 37; see also Ahlstrom, "Theology in America," 239.

> way becoming qualified for an happy reign in life, after we are delivered from death, essentially supposes the *use of means*, and such too as are proper to be used with moral agents.[65]

If one were diligent in attendance on the means of grace and lived a moral life in accordance with God's law, he could be assured that God would work grace in him. All that remained was for him to wait patiently for that work to progress.[66]

> In one sense Chauncy's approach represented a logical outcome of the whole New England apparatus of 'preparation for salvation'. If one were to devote oneself to attendance on the 'means of grace' in the hope of receiving the gift of salvation, did it not stand to reason that the means ought to guarantee what they claimed to provide? Chauncy thought so.[67]

Chauncy did not seem to recognize that this was relying on one's own works instead of relying on Christ. After all, according to Chauncy, Christ's work was indispensable to salvation.[68] In the sermon, "The New Creation Describ'd," Chauncy's unwitting movement can be discerned. Like many other sincere Puritans of his time, he opposed mere mental assent to truth[69] while practically equating a correct estimation of good things with faith, or at least making such an estimation one of the tests of faith and new life.

The prominent position of "evidences" in achieving assurance of salvation was a standard Puritan tenet, hardly lacking in evangelicals down to the present. The problem is that all the criteria offered to evaluate one's state of grace can be imitated by the flesh. Puritans greatly feared such an outcome and worked almost desperately at inward examination to insure their sincerity before God. However, the more one strives to be acceptable to God, the farther

---

65. Chauncy, *Mystery Hid*, 85; italics original.

66. Walker, *Ten New England Leaders*, 284; Lippy, *Seasonable Revolutionary*, 29–33.

67. Lippy, *Seasonable Revolutionary*, 119.

68. Chauncy, "Ministers Exhorted," 21–22.

69. Ahlstrom, *Religious History*, 131–32.

Charles Chauncy and the Liberal Position

he is from resting in Christ, even as a believer. The torturous results of this exacting examination are by no means confined to the Puritans. Puritans, like many since, went one of two ways—emotional experience or rational resolution. Charles Chauncy chose the latter.

As noted before, Puritans were overwhelmingly preoccupied with assurance of salvation, and Chauncy clearly reflects such emphasis. The vast majority of Chauncy's printed sermons and treatises deal with soteriological questions. During the Great Awakening both the pro-revivalists and their ecclesiastical opponents emphasized the individual in salvation, addressing the deep concerns for personal assurance of salvation, though from different viewpoints.[70] Chauncy's answers to the twofold soteriological question of the Great Awakening reveal a distinct Arminianism. Man by reason chooses whether or not to give logical assent to the truths (note the plural rather than the singular) of Christianity and to accept or reject the assistance of God's Spirit. If a person decides for the scriptural truths and the Spirit's assistance, he will lead an upright life in communion with the visible church. A person should examine himself to be certain that he continues to decide in favor of Christ wholeheartedly. Faith is essential according to Chauncy, but is not mysteriously imparted from on high.[71] Instead it is born of a close cooperation of the mind of man with the Spirit of God.[72] Well before Chauncy, New England Puritans had begun to teach that "faith does not require acquiescence to irrationalities, but empowers us to believe thoroughly in that which we can also accept intellectually. Faith is not intoxication, it is education."[73] Good works and good thoughts are sufficient evidences of faith. The impress of Perkins's teaching is unmistakable; Chauncy went further than his forebearers without a real disjunction with them.

This soteriological focus, which had been developing within colonial Puritan theology, necessarily affected Chauncy's view of God's nature. "The very fact that God allows himself to become

---

70. Lippy, *Seasonable Revolutionary*, 29–33; Nichols, *History of Christianity*, 76.

71. Chauncy, *Twelve Sermons*, 123–24.

72. Ahlstrom, "Theology in America," 240.

73. Miller, "Marrow of Puritan Divinity," 30.

committed to his creature must be in itself some indication of his essential disposition. Hence, if God condescends to treat with fallen man as with an equal [their concept of covenant theology], God must be a kindly and solicitous being."[74] The God to whom reason and nature pointed was a good and benevolent Creator. With this prominent feature of Enlightenment theology as a given, Chauncy understood traditional Puritan terms from a new angle. For example, Puritans had long emphasized the glory of God as a component of the chief end of man. Charles Chauncy (and others) simply defined the glory of God as primarily consisting in the happiness of creation.[75] "Religion came to be less a way of reconciliation with God and more the path to virtue and happiness, whereas the church existed less to glorify God than to make good and useful citizens."[76]

God was first and foremost benevolent. From this attribute stemmed not only all his other divine attributes, but also the creation and salvation of the world. While Chauncy proceeded to attempt working through the results or effects of this teaching on all other major doctrines, once settled on this point, he never thought further on the nature of God. With diligent effort, all Puritan doctrines could be redefined by this principle. Although Chauncy knew he was rethinking his doctrinal stand, in the light of reason and Scripture as he believed,[77] he never considered himself as truly altering the doctrine he had received.

Charles Chauncy's conclusions were, no doubt, in a direct line with Puritanism's departure from Calvinism; but the results of those conclusions no early Puritan would have been willing to accept. For Chauncy the most pressing question was "Is it reasonable?" Scripture could always be made to accommodate.

74. Miller, "Marrow of Puritan Divinity," 22.
75. Chauncy, *Benevolence*, 202–3; Lippy, *Seasonable Revolutionary*, 113.
76. Nichols, *History of Christianity*, 97.
77. Chauncy, *Mystery Hid*, v–xiv.

Mind over Scripture

Yes, correct use of reason came first and last and in between. However, the main point was not the use of reason as an instrument that was well-tuned and properly operated. Reason, that is man's natural, God-given faculty, possessed a type of self-existence related to the will and supposedly was in charge of the will—if properly cultivated. In this relative self-existence, reason might be treated as infallible. By no means did Charles Chauncy invent such a concept. He rather imbibed it in the writings of English rationalists and proponents of natural theology.

If reason were correctly applied to Scripture, which Charles Chauncy firmly believed to be inerrant and inspired, then the results understandably would yield right doctrine, which is saving truth.[78] Thus the interpretation of Scripture equaled Scripture in authority and importance. Chauncy readily accepted this implication of rationalistic religion. Men could (ought to) understand all that pertained to religion, no matter if some aspects of God's operations stood at such a great magnitude they required faith to affirm. These aspects in the end were not highly important because they did not pertain to salvation or life on earth. Chauncy questioned whether it was right or proper for man to investigate anything that did not appertain to his own business in this life and the next. Human experience, long a central concern in Puritan spirituality,[79] became definitive for rationalist theologians, including Chauncy.

Part and parcel of this experience was the physical creation. By observing the created order, man perceived that it must have a Creator and that he must be wise, benevolent, and good. Upon these principles man must both arrange his own life and direct his thoughts to admiring the Creator. Scripture was indispensable as the revelation of salvation, but creation should be also considered an indispensable part of the revelation of God.[80]

Although nature had been taught as the general revelation of God since the ancient church (a teaching accepted and employed

---

78. Chauncy, "Ministers Exhorted," 16–18.
79. Toon, *Emergence of Hyper-Calvinism*, 17.
80. Chauncy, *Benevolence*, 52–53.

by the Protestant Reformers), Enlightenment theologians exalted nature to a place which Calvin denied it,[81] that of being equal to Scripture in terms of its ability to reveal God. Not only did the rational religion to which Charles Chauncy subscribed highly exalt creation, it assigned general revelation, like many other features of orthodox Christianity, a new definition. The Reformers believed the accurate revelation of God in creation consisted of its reflection of its Creator. The rationalists, however, believed the accurate revelation of God in nature consisted of man's perception of the Creator as reflected in his creation. Man's observation of the physical world began to be treated as infallible revelation. Thus God could be known through science.[82]

Chauncy tried to use both science and mathematics in explaining God's essence and his works. Unfortunately for his ideas, these claims had been refuted already in ancient church teaching. Yet the ancient fathers, for all their wisdom, had little or no influence with proponents of rational theology. During the ancient times men must have been benighted, their light of reason suppressed by blind submission to the teaching of faith, since they had not come to the conclusion of the rationalists regarding God's essence and man's ability. Thus current thought was superior to the Rule of Faith. Since modern man was exercising his reasoning ability to the full potential, modern conclusions must necessarily be correct. The mechanical fatalism in these prideful ideas ironically went undetected even by the great minds of that school of thought.

> The Puritans were certain that the new inventions would not undermine their predispositions; as a result, they felt no qualms in examining and defending the new sciences. A new divinity,[83] natural law, was being erected alongside the Puritan God, but they did not realize it. It was not long before this new 'being' was to dominate religious thought.[84]

81. Calvin, *Institutes*, 11.6.4.

82. Madueme, "Adam and Evolution."

83. This "new divinity" should not be confused with Jonathan Edwards's successors.

84. Linden, "Charles Chauncy," 5.

Charles Chauncy and the Liberal Position

In his sermons and treatises, Chauncy often used the same terms as older Puritan writers but with slightly modified meanings that appear only after careful examination of the context in which he employs those terms.[85] To assume that Chauncy deliberately redefined Puritan terms and carefully slipped those into his preaching would be both unfair to Chauncy and also a grave mistake, overlooking the subtlety of anthropocentric reasoning today. Sincerity is an assistant, but it is not a safeguard. Confidence in sincerity alone is a danger. Praying is necessary, but watching is likewise required.[86]

In his early ministry Chauncy may not have perceived the difference between his teaching and that of Tudor-era Puritanism, but in his later years he did realize that he was considered unorthodox by many of his contemporaries, a charge he believed unfounded.[87] He had simply taken the Puritan theology that he had received to its logical end, or so he thought.[88] Most of New England thought so too.

---

85. See Chauncy, "Ministers Exhorted."
86. Matt 26:41.
87. Walker, *Ten New England Leaders*, 309–10.
88. Linden, "Charles Chauncy," 115.

Chapter 6

John Gill and the Conservative Position

Effects of the Enlightenment

Not all thinkers of the seventeenth and eighteenth centuries came to the same conclusions as Charles Chauncy on either reason's ability or the results of applying thorough thought to Christian doctrine. On the other side of the debate, on the other side of the Atlantic, stood John Gill.

JOHN GILL (1697–1771)

His Life and Controversies

Born in Kettering, England, to Particular Baptist parents,[1] John Gill eagerly entered grammar school at age eight, only to be forced to leave a few years later as the head-master insisted that all the boys under his charge attend Anglican services with him weekly.[2]

---

1. Anonymous, "Summary of the Life," ix.
2. Anonymous, "Summary of the Life," xi.

John Gill and the Conservative Position

Pressure on Non-conformists had greatly diminished in England by this time, but they still had no legal or scholastic recourse. Although not yet converted, John Gill personally held to his parents' convictions and relinquished his beloved school without resentment—remarkable at such a young age.

He did not give up studying on his own, however, while helping in his father's shop.[3] The Gills supported their son in his pursuits, believing that he would one day become a preacher and a champion of the gospel.[4] As Baptist ministers of the area became aware of John Gill's predicament and his dedication to learning, they gladly loaned him books from their personal libraries and provided brief tutoring sessions.[5] Thus, soon after John Gill made his faith public by baptism at the age of nineteen, he was asked to assist a Baptist congregation that was without a pastor in a nearby town. Called to a permanent pastorate in 1719, John Gill pastored for over fifty years at Horselydown in Southwark, London.[6]

Baptists at this time enjoyed increasingly stable political conditions. Nonetheless, doctrinal attack persisted from without only to be aggravated by doctrinal dissensions from within.[7] As a result John Gill faced a nearly continuous stream of controversies throughout his ministry, although, like Charles Chauncy, only one dispute was of great magnitude.

This grave controversy disturbed the ecclesiastical peace of England for almost one hundred years, vexing the established and dissenting churches alike.[8] The doctrine of the Trinity underwent some of the earliest and most sustained attacks of Enlightenment thinking. Most attackers advocated various forms of Arian Unitarianism. The anti-Trinitarians considered the doctrine of the Trinity to be confused, unessential, and even irrational.[9] Known as the

---

3. Anonymous, "Summary of the Life," xi.
4. Anonymous, "Summary of the Life," ix–x.
5. Anonymous, "Summary of the Life," x.
6. Anonymous, "Summary of the Life," xiv.
7. Oliver, "John Gill," 146.
8. Toon, *Emergence of Hyper-Calvinism*, 36–37.
9. Lim, *Mystery Unveiled*, 16, 183–84.

Socinian controversy, it was gradually abandoned by the Anglican Church and also was slighted by those who advocated political leniency and ecclesiastical egalitarianism. Thus the Reformed churches, chiefly represented in England by the Presbyterians and the Reformed Baptists, remained to defend the doctrine of the Trinity against the scoffers. Unfortunately, some Baptists began propounding the opposite heresy named Sabellianism.[10]

In this, as in many lesser controversies, John Gill became the Particular Baptist champion of his day.[11] In a dissertation written specifically on the doctrine of the Trinity and also in numerous sermons and tracts, Gill strove to defend the orthodox doctrine of the ancient creeds from the bases of the Scripture, the fathers, and reason. That threefold method, rooted firmly in Puritan tradition, was Gill's *modus operandi* in all his writings.[12] For example,

> Now since it appears that all the sound and orthodox writers have unanimously declared for the eternal generation and Sonship of Christ in all ages, and that those only of an unsound mind and judgment, and corrupt in others things as well as this . . . have declared against it, such must be guilty of great temerity and rashness to join in an opposition with the one against the other; and to oppose a doctrine the church of God has always held, and especially being what the scriptures [sic] abundantly bear testimony unto.[13]

John Gill never withdrew from private study, becoming at length renowned for his knowledge of Scripture as well as the original languages and rabbinical literature. In 1748 Marischal College and the University of Aberdeen granted Gill a Doctorate of Divinity in recognition of these accomplishments.[14] From this study and motivated by the danger which heresies and schisms presented to the church of God, including the flock over which he had the

---

10. Oliver, "John Gill," 153.
11. Anonymous, "Summary of the Life," xv–xvi, xxii.
12. Sant, "John Gill," 9.
13. Gill, "Dissertation Concerning the Eternal Sonship of Christ," 564.
14. Anonymous, "Summary of the Life," xxiii.

John Gill and the Conservative Position

oversight, Gill produced a great amount of exegetical, doctrinal, and apologetical writing.

John Gill's exegetical writings are comprised of his weighty *Body of Divinity*[15] and his widely influential and enduring commentary on the whole Bible, as well as many of his sermons. Gill's polemic and apologetic writings primarily concern the defense of the doctrines of credo-baptism, predestination, and the authority of the Bible. Obviously these are minor in comparison with the more serious controversy regarding the doctrine of the Trinity, but they are also minor in the number of participants. By Gill's later life the effects of the Enlightenment were telling in the rapid secularization of Europe and England in particular.[16] Less obvious, and for this reason perhaps more dangerous, were the effects of the Enlightenment on stout defenders of orthodoxy like John Gill.

Puritan Heritage of the Particular Baptists

Some may be shocked to learn that the Particular Baptists were the spiritual descendants of English Puritanism[17] that had divided into three strands: Anglicans, Non-conformists (Dissenters), and heretics. The Particular Baptists number among the Dissenters. Like other Puritans, the Particular Baptists did not all fall into error. Nevertheless, the more subtle doctrinal defects present in Puritanism and in other English Reformation traditions were also present in the Particular Baptist theology.[18]

---

15. McBeth, *Sourcebook for Baptist Heritage*, 117.
16. See Nichols, *History of Christianity*.
17. D'Aubingé, *History of the Reformation of the Sixteenth Century*, iv.
18. McBeth, *Sourcebook for Baptist Heritage*, 11.

GILL'S MATURE TEACHINGS ON GOD'S ONTOLOGY

His Commitment to the Doctrine of the Trinity

A final confession of the faith written to a friend shortly before his death demonstrates Gill's deep and lasting commitment to the Holy Trinity as well as his wariness of a prideful estimation of human ability.

> I depend wholly and alone upon the free sovereign, eternal, unchangeable and everlasting love of God; the firm and everlasting covenant of grace, and my interest in the persons of the Trinity; for my whole salvation: and not upon any righteousness of my own, nor any thing in me, or done by me under the influences of the holy [sic] Spirit; nor upon any services of mine, which I have been assisted to perform for the good of the church; but upon my interest in the persons of the Trinity, the person, blood and righteousness of Christ, the free grace of God, and the blessings of grace streaming to me through the blood and righteousness of Christ; as the ground of my hope. These are no new things with me; but what I have been long acquainted with; what I can live and die by. And this you may tell to any of my friends.[19]

While Charles Chauncy's treatment of Jesus' relationship to the Father was a secondary issue in his work *The Mystery Hid* (the most that relationship is ever discussed in his writings), John Gill vigorously taught and defended the doctrine of one holy, blessed, and undivided Trinity, writing on the doctrine as a whole and the eternal generation of the Son in particular.[20] What could possibly be faulty with Gill's trinitarian theology?

Unfortunately, Gill followed in the steps and, consequently, the errors of the early orthodox Puritans by emphasizing God's work over God's nature. Among God's works redemption ranks foremost. Therefore soteriology received a great deal of Gill's attention.

---

19. Anonymous, "Summary of the Life," xxxii.
20. Gill, *Doctrine of the Trinity.*

John Gill and the Conservative Position

That a pastor such as Gill should spend most of his time and effort instructing men in the way of salvation might seem natural and fitting. While undoubtedly a fine line exists in how much teaching should be devoted to salvation and sanctification versus other doctrines, unless Christ is preached in his essence, especially as a person of the Godhead, soteriology takes on an anthropocentric focus. Christ may not be preached for Christ's sake as much as for man's need. Again, the distinction may be regarded as minor or, by some, illusionary, but it is real and crucial. Let Christians take warning: if a man like Charles Chauncy fell into this, anyone could; and if a man like John Gill did, probably every orthodox believer likewise could discover elements of these problems in his own theology. "If the gold rusts, what will the iron do?"[21]

God's Work Emphasized over God's Nature

As with some other Reformation theologies, the basis of Puritan soteriology was the Covenant of Redemption,[22] which was based on God's decrees. These decrees, pertaining as they did to the ordering of human history, became inseparable in Puritan teaching from the persons whose destiny the decrees determined.[23] Looking at the deity from the perspective of man's destiny terribly skewed the perception of God's nature. Thus, soteriology became anthropocentric in spite of the teachers' intense desire for the glory of God.

In some ways, by consistently returning to the Savior, John Gill managed to avoid the grotesque caricature of the sovereign God that Puritan and other hyper-Calvinist doctrines developed. The sweetness and beauty of Christ filled his soul with a worship that is reflected in his writings. Gill perceived the love of the Father for the elect;[24] but because man's relationship to God predominated

---

21. Chaucer, "Canterbury Tales," 75.

22. Toon, *Emergence of Hyper-Calvinism*, 20; see also Gill, *Doctrine of Justification by the Righteousness of Christ*, 47–48.

23. Toon, *Emergence of Hyper-Calvinism*, 13–14.

24. Gill, *Doctrines of God's Everlasting Love*, 56–63.

over Christ's relation to the Father in Gill's thinking, even he succumbed to misconceptions of God's sovereignty.

If Charles Chauncy considered benevolence as the basic essence of God, John Gill, like many orthodox Puritans, considered sovereignty as the basic definition of God rather than triunity. So prominently did the Puritans' concept of God's eternal decrees figure in their theology that the descriptions given of his work among men developed a rather detached sound.[25] John Gill carefully taught the believer's mystical union with Christ in all its eternal vitality.[26] Nevertheless, his teaching appears to have become compartmentalized.

When discussing who would be saved and how, Gill portrays the outworking of God's secret counsels quite mechanistically,[27] in keeping, of course, with the Puritan tradition he had received. Such a mechanistic interpretation had partially arisen due to the reading of time back into eternity past. The problem was not in teaching that all happenings occurred as ordered in God's secret counsels before the world was created,[28] but in not leaving the workings of those counsels a secret.

Long before the time of John Gill, the effects of divine foreknowledge and predestination had been ascribed to the individual decrees of God in eternity past and then been assigned a specific sequence.[29] Both Sub- and Supra-lapsarians (so named for their minor disagreement on the exact order of these decrees) believed that the teaching of Scripture necessitated such an ordering. John Gill was a Supra-lapsarian who recognized that the differences between his position and that of the Sub-lapsarians were indeed minor.[30] His writings work out some of the logical results of the Supra-lapsarian system. In so doing, he incorporates many accurate statements regarding God's sovereignty. At the same time he can cause it to

25. Toon, *Emergence of Hyper-Calvinism*, 22.
26. Gill, *Doctrines of God's Everlasting Love*, 6–13.
27. Gill, *Cause of God and Truth*, 3.5.13.2.
28. Eph 1:3–12.
29. Toon, *Emergence of Hyper-Calvinism*, 13–14.
30. Gill, *Cause of God and Truth*, 3.1.5.1.

John Gill and the Conservative Position

appear as if God's decrees, now instituted, were functioning on their own.[31] God's sovereignty was in danger of being detached from God's essence.[32]

While not all that John Gill wrote had a soteriological emphasis (for example, his other doctrinal writings noted above), soteriology, as expressed in the Covenant of Redemption, formed the backbone of his theology,[33] as it did for many Reformed and evangelicals then and since. The direct relation of the Father to man and the rest of creation, indeed the direct Creator-creature relations of the entire Godhead as such, prominent in Calvin's writings, had been exchanged for a focus on Christ's mediatory role.[34] This may be familiar from the Charles Chauncy discussion; and while John Gill never took this view to the heretical end that Charles Chauncy did,[35] nevertheless the shift of focus impacted both his soteriology and the doctrine of the Trinity.

The subordination implicit in the Puritan interpretation of the Covenant of Redemption is present in Gill's writings although no more explicit there than in former writers. Christ's willing submission to the Father's demands and propositions jeopardizes the unity of the Godhead. The idea of covenant is largely equivalent to a contract.[36] Gill suggests the Godhead as three minds conferring.[37] "The Father made the covenant; the Son is become the Surety, Mediator, and Messenger of it; and the Spirit of God stands by, as a witness to it; and to see all the articles agreed upon between the Father and the Son, perform'd on each side."[38] The difficulty with visualizing Christ as receiving a commission from the Father in eternity past is that it views Christ, not as equal to the Father, but

---

31. Gill, *Complete Body of Doctrinal and Practical Divinity*, 1.2.2.

32. Gill, *Cause of God and Truth*, 3.1.2.2, 3.7.1.5.

33. Gill, *Doctrines of God's Everlasting Love*, 45–61.

34. Gill, *Doctrines of God's Everlasting Love*, 31, 40–41, 47; see also Gill, *Complete Body of Doctrinal and Practical Divinity*, 1.2.13.3.

35. Toon, *Emergence of Hyper-Calvinism*, 108.

36. Gill, *Doctrine of the Trinity*, 63–68; see also Gill, *Doctrines of God's Everlasting Love*, 52–53.

37. Gill, *Justification by the Righteousness of Christ*, 9–12.

38. Gill, *Doctrine of the Trinity*, 63–64.

subject to him as if already in the state of humiliation enacted at the incarnation.[39]

Gill is in great danger of designating the Trinity "Creator, Redeemer, Sanctifier"[40] like the modern theology that assigns a specific role to each of the persons of the Trinity. This view of the Trinity designates each person by the work that is chiefly his in the economy of grace, rather than titling each person by his proper name. In this perspective each person has an individual work that coordinates with the work of the other two persons. Instead of the divine movements being inseparable from the divine nature of the Trinity proceeding and receiving definition from the nature of God, each person becomes defined by a function from which he is inseparable. Although Gill strives to avoid this conclusion, it appears repeatedly in his discussion of each person of the Trinity.[41]

The Subtle Influence of Rationalism

In writing his defense of the doctrine of the Trinity, Gill observed

> That it is a doctrine of great importance, needs no other evidence, tho' other may easily be given, than the great opposition which satan [sic] has made against it. He, indeed, has recourse to many stratagems, wiles, and cunning devises to support his own interest, and hurt the interest of Christ.... One is, ... to magnify and exalt the reason of man, his intellectual powers, and the freedom of his will, in spiritual and divine things.[42]

How could a person this insightful into the origin and danger of rationalism be rationalistic? In the answer to that question lies the warning for all. Like many of his day,[43] John Gill fell prey to the desire to demonstrate with reasons why he believed what he

---

39. Gill, *Justification by the Righteousness of Christ*, 52–54.
40. See also chapter 7.
41. Gill, *Doctrine of the Trinity*.
42. Gill, *Doctrine of the Trinity*, 3.
43. May, *Enlightenment in America*, 13.

John Gill and the Conservative Position

did. Attempting to give an answer for the faith,[44] he slipped into attempting to convince the natural man of spiritual things.[45] To accomplish this, spiritual subjects had to be explained in naturally rational terms. These terms obscured the truth instead of elucidating it because they were not of the same nature as the subject. They were an earth shadow on the sky.

Perhaps this slip is most obvious in Gill's defense of the authority of Scripture itself.[46] Calvin had specifically warned against nearly all of the proofs Gill brought forward. Calvin demonstrated that, while evidences of the superiority of Scripture and its divine origin are appropriate and comfortable to a believer, they should never be accepted as proofs or depended upon to support Scripture. Outside evidences of the superior and divine origin of Scripture are based on human reasoning and perception. Concerning questions of faith, as Calvin pointed out, this is shifting sand. His prediction bore out as rational explanations of the faith failed to be sufficient for either the skeptics or for the weak in the faith. Only the Spirit's inward testimony and work of speaking through Scripture offer a solid rock for faith.[47] As Perry Miller states, the Puritans sensed the need to give rationalistic framework to their doctrines.[48] Indeed, rationalism was already on the rise in Calvin's day and far from escaping his notice.[49] However, Calvin perceived its vanity, calling it sophistry.

John Gill's rational defense of Scripture provides a clue to his understanding of the relation of Scripture to interpretation and to nature. Obviously, Gill honored Scripture and was renowned for his dedication to its study. Even more than Charles Chauncy, John Gill strongly desired to be scriptural. He believed Scripture to be far above man's reason in power and authority as the revelation of God. Nevertheless, Gill overlooked the fact that in trying to offer a

---

44. 1 Pet 3:15.
45. Gill, *Doctrine of the Trinity*, 6.
46. Gill, *Complete Body of Doctrinal and Practical Divinity*, 1.1.2.
47. Calvin, *Institutes*, 1.1.7.4–5, 1.1.9.13.
48. Miller, "Marrow of Puritan Divinity," 30.
49. Calvin, *Institutes*, 1.1.5.4.

primarily rational defense of Scripture and doctrine rather than a primarily spiritual answer, he had conceded to humanistic reason's claim to sit in judgment on spiritual questions from outside of the orthodox Christian faith. Such an approach was to treat Scripture as dependent upon reason instead of reason as dependent upon Scripture. In short, "Is it reasonable?" was as important, though not more important than, "Is it scriptural?"

Just as John Gill was unconscious of the place he had afforded man's nature in the form of unaided reason, he seems to have been equally unaware of the status he gave interpretation in relation to the Scriptures themselves. Thoroughly affected by the mechanistic view of scriptural interpretation prevalent to this day, John Gill argued against the Arminians based on Supra-lapsarian views as a given as much as the Scriptures.[50]

Such an argument brings to light another clue: Sweet reasonableness is deceitful, especially in debate. John Gill somewhat uncomfortably took a position on the outworking of God's will when cornered there by the questions and assertions of the Arminians with whom he was debating.[51] In doing this he, like others of his day, took up questions Calvin regarded as unwise. Perhaps no better example exists of how hyper-Calvinism went beyond Calvinism than all of the following warnings that were disregarded: against assigning order to God's eternal decrees, against basing faith on arguments of reason, and finally, against giving thought to questions that ought not have that sort of respect. The lesson holds true today.

---

50. Gill, *Cause of God and Truth*, 3.1.2.3.
51. Gill, *Cause of God and Truth*, 3.2.1.2.

Chapter 7

Becoming Theocentric

CENTRALITY OF CHARITY—THINKING OF GOD AS SOVEREIGN FROM AN ONTOLOGICALLY TRINITARIAN PERSPECTIVE

Putting Reason in the Picture (Love of God)

"Thou shalt love the Lord thy God with all thy heart, and with all thy soul, and with all thy mind."[1] Every part of man, including his reason, was created by God and obtains its fulfillment only in God. Interestingly, Augustine did not consider the reason to be its own entity within man as the Enlightenment thinkers did, but as a faculty of the soul, enabling the soul to press toward God in understanding and fellowship.[2] Ecstasy would not suffice. Energetic effort on the part of the soul was required to know the God who had revealed himself faintly in creation, clearly in Scripture, then finally and definitely in the incarnation of the Lord Jesus Christ. Augustine's view

---

1. Matt 22:37.
2. Augustine, "Soliloquies," 358–60.

may be summed up in Christ's own words, "worship *him* [God] in spirit and in truth."[3] These are the keys to the kingdom.

God can only be known and hence loved as he reveals himself to man. God's ontology is the basis for theology. The inability of man to perceive saving truth from the testimony of creation is starkly evidenced by the universal prevalence of paganism.[4] Scripture alone can fully reveal to man God's nature as clearly as it reveals his works. Nevertheless Scripture remains a closed book to man until illuminated by the Holy Spirit, God himself speaking through his word. "Verily thou *art* a God that hidest thyself, O God of Israel, the Saviour."[5] The unaided intellect, no matter how acute, cannot discern truth on its own from Scripture or creation.

The Spirit that enlightens believers is the Spirit of Christ[6] sent by Christ from the Father and equal with both in the Godhead. Only as man recognizes the Godhead in Christ, properly relating the persons to each other, will he be able to perceive the truth about God's character and nature. Any misconceptions about the relations of the Father to the Son and of either to the Spirit will eventually result in a misconception of God's nature and sovereignty over his creation. A correct Christology is indispensable to a true theology. Man can only understand God's true view of man in the Father's view of Christ. "Any anthropocentric conception of man is refuted by the assertion of a radically Christocentric anthropology."[7]

However, as a believer contemplates Christ through the Spirit's light on the Scriptures, he will develop a humble confidence in God's guidance. God did provide the Scriptures. Christ did become incarnate, "taking of the manhood into God."[8] The Spirit did descend upon the church as promised. God has sought and found the lost sheep. Now he will lead by the green pastures and still waters of his own revelation.

3. John 4:23-24.
4. Calvin, *Institutes*, 1.1-2. See Rom 1.
5. Isa 45:15.
6. Rom 8:9; 1 Pet 1:11.
7. Timiadis, *Nicene Creed*, 39.
8. The Athanasian Creed; see appendix.

Becoming Theocentric

To fully rest in God's guidance, however, a believer must relinquish human evaluation. This relinquishing is twofold. On the one hand, he cannot entertain an overly exalted view of the abilities of his own reason. Human reason is not a mechanical processor into which pieces of Scripture can be poured to yield a smooth, accurate doctrine. Reason, at its best, is fallible, and therefore cannot be relied upon when dealing with truth. Resting in God's guidance means that, in addition to fully expecting God to work his gracious will in the believer in Christ, all other rests are abandoned.

On the other hand, releasing human evaluation has another, more challenging aspect, namely, disregarding the criticisms and contempt of carnal men concerning the believer's lowered esteem of human reason. Few temptations are as powerful as the temptation to appear wise, especially in spiritual matters, as our first parents learned in the garden of Eden. No change has taken place since then except that the fallen nature has greater susceptibility. The beauty of holding the truth in humility is best observed from the outside, although such a position is often feared and therefore hated by unbelievers. During the time of his humiliation, Christ, who is the Truth, said the world would always be thus.[9] However "the fear of man bringeth a snare" that is unavoidable.[10] Strangely enough, this fear is itself unreasonable, as all wrong fears are.

At the same time, however, a believer must be diligent in interpretation. Reason cannot remain idly by while the other faculties of man are employed in the worship of God. The Scriptures themselves declare that God expects man, a believer especially, to apply the mind he gave him, not as if independent from God, but in his service. Faith without thought is no more than emotionalism.

Human reason is not master of the Scriptures but a steward who will have to give an account of his stewardship.[11]

> The main stream of Christian theology has been neither rationalistic nor irrationalistic. It is ready to give full weight to the truth for which Liberalism has

---

9. John 15:18, 24–25; 17:14.
10. Prov 29:25.
11. 1 Cor 4:1–2.

contended—namely, that the human reason is a God-given faculty having full rights in its own proper sphere and under proper control, but it is free from the subjectivism and ephemerality to which Liberalism is exposed. It refuses to agree with Liberalism that the terrain of theology must be cleared of the accumulated work of nearly two millennia in order that, on the bare earth of natural reason, there may be erected an entirely new theological edifice to twentieth-century [or twenty-first century] specifications.[12]

Having been commanded to think[13] and to search the Scriptures,[14] no believer ought to rely on mere emotion. Only the obedient believer has true claim to faith.[15] Therefore, to whatever degree a believer strives to think and search the Scriptures, he is exhibiting faith. On the other hand, the believer that attempts to worship God solely with emotion is not evidencing faith in that area.

Furthermore, in addition to explicit statements, the Scriptures contain implicit directives for interpretation. "Comparing spiritual things with spiritual"[16] presupposes the exercise of reason, a well-developed reason that may be termed *discernment*.[17] As stated above, spiritual discernment is not a function of man's unaided reason; rather it is the evidence that reason is serving God in its rightful place. "This means that there is a permanent duty incumbent upon the Church's leaders and thinkers to rectify and verify all developments in practice and doctrine by the standard of the apostolic tradition,"[18] in other words, the Rule of Faith.

12. Mascall, *Christ, the Christian, and the Church*, 246.
13. Phil 4:8.
14. John 5:39.
15. Jas 2:17–26.
16. 1 Cor 2:13.
17. Mal 3:18; Heb 5:14.
18. Mascall, *Christ, the Christian, and the Church*, 242.

Putting Experience in the Picture (Love of the Brethren[19])

Scripture is likewise explicit that serving God with the mind is only the first step. One must also serve another in love.[20] Edification of other believers includes not only right use of the Scriptures, but also proper use of experience. Spiritual experiences with God and other believers are not to be despised anymore than they are to be overrated. "If I am not mistaken, the doctrine of the Trinity suffers more than other central doctrines of the Christian creed from not being thus closely related to the practice of the Christian religion. This need not be so."[21]

In order to employ experience correctly, it must be subjected to the Scriptures. Experience is revelation put into practice. Only as an experience is understood in light of Scripture can it have true spiritual use. In and of themselves, spiritual experiences will most likely lead believers astray.[22] Believers must not think that "in the fear of God lies all wisdom, and if you are wise you cannot ever err."[23] During the Great Awakening, Charles Chauncy, similar to many other New England pastors, suffered censorious judgment at the hands of those who believed their relative experiences granted them the wherewithal to determine another's state of grace.[24] Obviously such attitudes demonstrate a lack of charity, disregarding the central place the Scriptures afford that virtue in all dealings with God and man:[25] "Love *is* the fulfilling of the law."[26]

In addition to being subject to the Scriptures, experience must be subject to reason, while reason operates as the steward of the Scriptures. "The spirits of the prophets are subject to the prophets."[27] All experience requires interpretation. It cannot simply stand on its

19. 1 Pet 1:22.
20. Gal 5:13; see also John 14–16.
21. Hodgson, *Doctrine of the Trinity*, 176.
22. Faust and Johnson, *Jonathan Edwards*, xxxvii.
23. Cervantes, *Don Quixote*, 767.
24. Lippy, *Seasonable Revolutionary*, 35.
25. 1 Cor 13.
26. Rom 13:10.
27. 1 Cor 14:32.

own. How one considers his experiences bears directly on how he will apply them. The foundational position of God's ontology to all spiritual thought has long been celebrated in worship.

> Men do not normally feel so deeply over matters of formal doctrinal statement unless those matters are felt to bear upon the practice of their piety. The close interrelation of doctrine and worship is an important element in explaining the desperate seriousness with which issues of doctrine were regarded in the early centuries.[28]

"GOD IS OUR GOD"[29]—VIEWING THE ECONOMIC TRINITY IN LIGHT OF ONTOLOGY

Since God has given man the Scriptures, given reason, given experience, and, above all, given Christ, how should God and his works be viewed? God's communication to man must be understood to be the communication of himself, not merely of a collection of facts. God's works must be contemplated in light of his nature. What a person believes concerning the one influences what he believes concerning the other. God does *what* he does because he is *who* he is.

What then is the definitive nature or ontology of God by which his works are to be understood? God is Trinity, one undivided Godhead of three co-equal and co-eternal persons. From the intra-relations of the Holy Trinity, God-as-God-is-in-himself, believers comprehend that "God is love."[30] Only in the holy and pure intensity of this selfless love of each person of the Godhead to each of the other persons can anyone understand the true essence of God.[31]

---

28. Wiles, *Making of Christian Doctrine*, 62.
29. Ps 48:14.
30. 1 John 4:8, 16.
31. Augustine, "On the Trinity," 37–42.

Becoming Theocentric

God Is Creator

This love created the world.[32] A right view of man, of society, and of the physical universe begins with a right view of the nature of the Creator—God as Trinity. Any reversal of that order will lead to varying levels of error in each view, depending on where in the doctrinal system the reversal occurs and to what degree the order is reversed. Charles Chauncy viewed God the Creator's nature from the perspective of man's nature and the physical universe, resulting in openly heretical views of God and man.[33] John Gill viewed God the Creator's nature from the perspective of God's self-revelation, but focused on how that revelation portrayed God's dealings with his chief creation, man. Gill's views of God's ontology could not truly be called heterodox.[34] However, the minor errors that they contained persist and in less able hands become magnified.[35]

God is man's Maker. The Father created man by his Word, who is his Son, and by the Holy Spirit. The Son and the Spirit share fully the initiative of the creative act. "Creator" is a proper title for God, one that he claims rightfully as his own;[36] but though it does not describe his essence, the title applies to all three persons. The modern attempt to term the persons of the Trinity "Creator, Redeemer, Sanctifier"[37] fails to acknowledge the authoritative activity of each of the persons of the Godhead in creation.

Many unbelievers, and sadly some believers, attack the role and title of God as Creator. Far from being a novel viewpoint or assertion, the denial of an independent, self-sufficient Creator by the application of anthropocentric rationale has existed from at least the time of the Greeks[38] and was revived by secular rationalists during the Enlightenment. Ironically, this proud denial only serves to demonstrate the apostle's words in Romans 1. The Creator's position

---

32. Toon, *Our Triune God*, 36.
33. Chauncy, *Mystery Hid*, vii–viii.
34. Toon, *Emergence of Hyper-Calvinism*, 108.
35. Oliver, "John Gill," 162.
36. Isa 43:15.
37. Toon, *Doctrine of the Trinity*. See also chapter 6.
38. Timiadis, *Nicene Creed*, 51.

may be clearly seen in creation, leaving man without excuse.[39] Nevertheless to fallen man, creation's testimony cannot communicate the spiritual wisdom and the illumination that would enable him to understand God accurately. The result of man's misconstruction of nature's truth is idolatry of one type or another, whether in physical or mental image.[40] Man makes God to be what man sees in himself and the rest of creation.

Natural theologians believe that the experience of God in nature, if responsibly interpreted, presents man a correct view of God. Modern examples include rationalism, romanticism, and even Hegelianism. Some Christians view natural theology as at least better than atheism, but such is not necessarily the case. To truly exalt God, man must relinquish his overly exalted view of himself. However, only a correct view of God will truly exalt him.

By virtue of God's place as Creator, he holds absolute authority over his creation. Notwithstanding, the position of Creator must be understood by the nature of the One who holds that position: This much Charles Chauncy did realize. However neither benevolence, sovereignty, nor any other attribute equals God's essence. At any time God can declare "I AM" and any of his revealed attributes could apply. However, God is not just a compilation of his attributes. "I AM" indicates his self-existence apart from any outside influence or dependence on any being outside himself, including his creation.[41]

However, God as the "I AM" has provided himself (his being) as the fulfillment of the souls he created.[42] God's place as Creator includes his place as Provider and Sustainer, summed up in the historic title of Providence. A serious dilemma arose, however, when Providence became an impersonal, abstract concept. God, the ever-blessed, Holy Trinity of three co-equal persons with each indwelling, loving, and exalting each other eternally, is far from an impersonal, cold, mental abstraction. A great deal of mental effort

---

39. Rom 1:20.
40. Calvin, *Institutes*, 1.1.5.11–15.
41. Exod 3:13–14.
42. Benjamin, *Simply Singular*, 36.

is required to correctly comprehend this from the teachings of Scripture. This is the God who created all things.

> Consider the lilies of the field, how they grow; they toil not, neither do they spin: and yet I say unto you, that even Solomon in all his glory was not arrayed like one of these. Wherefore, if God so clothed the grass of the field, which today is, and tomorrow is cast into the oven, *shall he* not much more *clothe* you, O ye of little faith?"[43]

Herein exists the paradox: faith is required to perceive the truth about God, but it has to be "faith seeking understanding."[44]

Creation is for edification[45] when thoughtfully considered with proper use of reason by the spiritually enlightened mind. "I consider thy heavens, the work of thy fingers, the moon and the stars, which thou hast ordained."[46] Numerous passages of Scripture, including our Lord's parables, draw on nature for examples in teaching spiritual truth. Many orthodox Puritans understood this point; contemplation of the natural world by the eye of faith yields delight in God.[47]

God Is Savior

"My spirit hath rejoiced in God my Saviour."[48] A believer's joy in God as Savior far outweighs his joy in God as Creator, provided, that is, that the concept of God's position as Redeemer is grounded in a proper view of God's nature. As noted in the discussion on John Gill, nowhere is the dedicated believer at greater risk of anthropocentric reasoning regarding God's nature than when considering soteriology. Multitudes of evangelicals, including the Reformed,

---

43. Matt 6:28–30.
44. Augustine, "Faith Seeking Understanding," 255–62.
45. 1 Tim 4:4; see also Timiadis, *Nicene Creed*, 49.
46. Ps 8:3.
47. St. John, *American Literature for Christian Schools*, 61.
48. Luke 1:47.

Earth Shadows on the Sky

emphasize how, when, and to whom the gospel should be preached to the relative neglect of the nature of the gospel's Source.

> Let us remember though that we are to believe in the deity of Christ not firstly because a divine Mediator is necessary for our salvation but because this doctrine is revealed in the Bible and is therefore true and authoritative, whether we are personally deriving saving benefit from it or not.
>
> It is this belief, along with that of the Trinity, that especially separates the true church of Christ from the range of deviant cults.[49]

Modern evangelicals, as Charles Chauncy and John Gill before them, often consider themselves Christ-centered because their main focus is on the salvation that Jesus accomplished for believers (according to their various interpretations of his part in man's redemption) when in reality they are man-centered, focusing on those who are to be saved instead of who Christ is.[50] "Chauncy had shifted the corner-stone of religious thought from a theocentric anthropology to an androcentric theology. . . . He simply began from a different starting point, rearranged and reformulated doctrinal explication, and arrived at an unorthodox destination."[51]

One of the errors, if not *the* major error, of Charles Chauncy and, to a certain extent, of John Gill is a mechanistic, legal-type interpretation of Christ's work as merely a transaction with the Father that mankind could not accomplish without him. They did not view the entire Trinity as working in concert to incorporate believers, organically and spiritually, into Christ through the Spirit in order to bring them into relationship and communion with the Father in the inner life of the Holy Trinity.[52]

Such a mechanistic, legal-type interpretation is prominent today. It is a kenotic Christology of varying levels of intensity that practically, though not theoretically, denies the thorough totality of

49. Blunt, "Which Bible Version?," 17.
50. Olson, *Westminster Handbook to Evangelical Theology*, 156, 260.
51. Lippy, *Seasonable Revolutionary*, 114.
52. Athanasius, "On the Incarnation," 65.

Becoming Theocentric

the hypostatic union.[53] Christ's essential unity with the Father must be understood before, during, and after the incarnation as well as believers' organic, spiritual union with Christ now and through all ages. The covenant is located in Christ rather than arranged with him.[54] No give-and-take is involved in the Trinity. The will of the Godhead is one, although possessed by all three persons.[55] The believer's inclusion through Christ into the life and love of the eternal Trinity is his salvation, hope, joy, and peace. Yet he must understand that life and love to some degree if he is to comprehend what is his in Christ. "God hath given to us eternal life, and this life is in his Son."[56]

Interestingly, when the Godhead is defined in terms of man's salvation, the Father's place in redemption is often minimized or neglected.[57] For many Protestants, Christ takes the place that the Roman Catholics assigned to the Virgin Mary, a tender protector who shields souls from the Father's Zeus-like wrath.[58] When these people endeavor to understand Christ's unity with the Father, they either attribute such wrath to Christ as well or reduce God's displeasure upon sin to a grandfatherly shake of the head, leaving man to grapple with the disastrous results of sin largely on his own. Those who focus on salvation will eventually try to manipulate God by using various means (whether sacraments, strict obedience to God's commands, or emotional services of worship) to make the Spirit work within themselves.

Having the Economic Trinity, God-as-God-is-toward-us, prominent is not necessarily anthropocentric as long as it remains attached to the Ontological Trinity, God-as-God-is-in-himself. Only in the true relations of Christ to the Father and the Spirit to Christ and the Father can soteriology and sovereignty be truly understood.

---

53. See glossary for definition.
54. Athanasius, "On the Incarnation," 40.
55. Athanasius, "Against the Heathen," 28–29.
56. 1 John 5:11.
57. Mascall, *Christ, the Christian, and the Church*, 88–89.
58. Shadley, "Leading Trinitarian Incarnational Worship," 3.

> If the church is to hold a doctrine of predestination as part of its confession that God alone is the author of salvation, then that doctrine must not exclude the doxological and prayer aspects. If the presentation of the ecclesiastical doctrine is such that it encourages speculation into God's eternal thoughts instead of worship of his nature, then it is not acceptable.[59]

When the Son who offered himself as a sacrifice is understood to be one with the Father who received the sacrifice, then the attitude of both toward those on whose behalf the sacrifice was offered may also be correctly perceived.[60] This means that at the cross both the Father and the Son displayed tender love and mercy toward sinful man.[61] There also, the Son, as much as the Father, demonstrated wrath against sin itself, together with its instruments. "God was in Christ, reconciling the world unto himself."[62] At the second advent, the results of divine reconciliation will be the Son's glorious display of wrath against the unrighteous and of redemption for those he has made righteous.[63]

Believers can only be joined to God because Christ is fully joined to both as noted above.[64] The Trinity may be termed Economic because saving grace flows from all three persons in the one Godhead.[65] In "Against the Arians," Athanasius refutes both halves of the Arian challenge: if God had a Son, was it by his will or by necessity?[66] As God is beyond the dichotomy of will versus necessity, the election and salvation of believers is not simply of necessity (Charles Chauncy) or of will (John Gill).

---

59. Toon, *Development of Doctrine in the Church*, 118.
60. Mascall, *Christ, the Christian, and the Church*, 75.
61. John 3:16.
62. 2 Cor 5:19.
63. 2 Thess 1:6–10.
64. Athanasius, "Against the Arians," 435–36.
65. Eph 3:14–21; Col 2:2.
66. Athanasius, "Against the Arians," 425–31.

Becoming Theocentric

God Is King

"The Lord *is* King for ever and ever."[67] "The Lord hath prepared his throne in the heavens."[68]

The sovereign Ruler of the universe directs and rules all his creation in love. Love to his creation includes hatred of and vengeance upon all that destroys that creation—Satan, sin, and evil men.[69] This is why he declares himself to be named Jealous: he cares for, protects, and keeps his own for himself. His elect are the apple of his eye.[70] The condemnation and the judgment on wickedness must be examined in light of the all-perfect love behind that judgment. This is not an arbitrary God who has the power to determine at random what shall or shall not be,[71] but a God who is himself the Source of all created reality. His being provides true meaning to persons, objects, and events, both inasmuch as that being is revealed and as it is ineffable. He is not a God whose benevolence forces him to grant man self-determination and then somehow rescue man from the results of that self-determination, but a God whose ways are past finding out because they differ from man's ways both in kind as well as magnitude.[72]

The carnal man rebels at the authority of God over him.[73] "We will not have this *man* to reign over us."[74] Nonetheless, invoking the unavoidability of God's decrees in response to man's rebellion may not necessarily be as spiritual as it first seems. If God's dealings with man can be thought of as "decrees" without separating these dealings from God's nature as Trinity, then the concept of "decrees" may be used. However, if the term "decrees" intrinsically indicates chronological order in eternity and an inverted view of the covenant, then it should be abandoned as a term. "Counsels" might

---

67. Ps 10:16.
68. Ps 103:19.
69. Lindblad, "Jesus Weeps."
70. Ps 17:8.
71. Toon, *Emergence of Hyper-Calvinism*, 54–55.
72. Rom 11:33; Job 9:10; Isa 55:8–11, especially v. 9.
73. Benjamin, *Simply Singular*, 29–30.
74. Luke 19:14.

be more explanatory[75] or another term might be desirable. God's sovereignty cannot be properly understood from his works: It must be understood by his essence as the Holy Trinity. If sovereignty and the doctrine of the Trinity appear to be unrelated, one's doctrines may possibly have become compartmentalized.

God is King, sovereign, because of his nature as God. God's nature is triune, and the Trinity rules over all in the economy of grace. The right response to God's authority (his sovereignty) is to humble oneself before him as Creator and to rest by faith in his goodness as the Creator who redeemed his own self-corrupting creation. This response is the evidence of grace at work in a soul and, hence, originates only from the presence of the Spirit who cannot be coerced. Nevertheless, the Spirit condescends to man gently, graciously, persistently. He, the Seven Eyes of the Lamb that sees (and therefore controls) everything in the earth,[76] enlightens the believer's eyes of understanding.[77]

Enlightenment has fascinated men, including Christians, since ancient times, resulting in Gnosticism, the Enlightenment era in the West, and spiritualism in the East and the West, both within and without the church. All of these approaches to enlightenment have resulted in personal and ecclesiastical unrest. Part of the rest in Christ as Shepherd, who is a Ruler and a Guide, is the assurance that the Spirit of Christ will direct believers in Christ through the written word. Although God rules without interference over the entire physical and spiritual creation, he especially rules over his church, which is his own people, his kingdom of priests.[78] Decent order in the church reflects and stems from God's divine, sovereign ordering of all things.[79] It is produced in the church by a firm, humble reliance on the normal function of the Scriptures as long as no artificial disjunction is placed between the word and the Spirit's application of the word.

75. Acts 2:23.
76. Rev 5:6; Zech 3:9, 4:10.
77. Eph 1:18.
78. 1 Pet 2:9.
79. 1 Cor 14:40.

Becoming Theocentric

In the name of the Lord Jesus Christ, believers ascertain his threefold claim to them. First, he stands as the authority to which all creation must answer. Moreover, as their Lord, they are under his special protection. (In this usage "King" and "Lord" are interchangeable.) By incorporating his elect into himself, Christ incorporated them into his kingdom, not merely as subjects but as kings.[80] Secondly, Jesus ("Jehovah saves") saves them as Jehovah, the only true God. Therefore the people of God belong to him. Thirdly, as 1 John declares, one cannot rightly worship or love God if he does not first believe that Jesus is the Christ, God in the flesh. Christ, the Anointed of God, is the sole access to God because he is himself God. He is also the one through whom God has revealed himself to humanity. Believers are under the headship of the Lord Jesus Christ because he is their King, their God, and their Savior.

The Beatific Vision[81]

Understanding God as Trinity can unveil a new world of spiritual thought, discerning who God is as well as what he does. In this new world, God appears more magnificent than ever before, more powerful, more sovereign, more transcendent, more divine. Howbeit, who he is provides the basis of all he does; God never acts out of character. Words fail to adequately or even accurately describe God. Yet he surpassed this seeming difficulty in revealing himself to man both in words and as the Word.[82] The Spirit opens to believers a new, deeper understanding of what Christ has accomplished and what believers possess in him. God-as-God-is-in-himself cannot be understood apart from God-as-God-is-toward-us, and vice versa. "For unless you first of all grasp what your relationship to God is, and the nature of his judgment concerning you, you have neither a foundation on which to establish your salvation nor one on which to build piety toward God."[83] God-as-God-is-in-himself should be

---

80. Hahn, *Kinship by Covenant*, 233.
81. See glossary for definition.
82. Augustine, "Faith Seeking Understanding," 256.
83. Calvin, *Institutes*, 1.3.11.1.

the foundation of a believer's understanding of God-as-God-is-toward-us. God is always the same,[84] but man's view of God will be impacted by which view of the Trinity (ontological or economical) is considered primary. Not only Arius and Charles Chauncy but also many today uphold the economic view to the complete obscurity of the ontological. Others today are like John Gill: they endeavor to maintain both views concurrently, but inevitably the ontological begins to slip. The economical must be held within the context of the ontological for both to be preserved.

Whichever import of the two views of the Trinity (how they relate or ought to be distinguished) is considered, the emphasis must remain on the persons of God, relating both to each other and to man and not merely to their activities. The Scriptures reveal how to express the truth about God in a manner acceptable to him. The church's struggle to confess scriptural faith demonstrates how to apply philosophical technique to theology without corrupting the doctrine of God with the doctrine of men. The fathers demonstrate how to reverently dare[85] to continue striving to construct a logical theory of God in accordance with the Scriptures. On the other hand, the post-Reformation Enlightenment era demonstrates the disastrous consequences of placing what God *does* above who God *is*.

The apostle Paul declares that the gospel, which may be equated with the entire New Testament, is the revelation of the mystery of God hidden from all past ages. What was that mystery? It was "that God was in Christ, reconciling the world unto himself."[86] The glorious unveiling of the Son of God is the reoccurring theme of the New Testament. The very title *New Testament* points to this; it is the new testament in the blood of Christ Jesus as he told the disciples at the Last Supper. Again the book of Hebrews states that Christ is the mediator of a new covenant and that a testament becomes effective only upon the death of the testator.[87]

84. Ps 102:27.
85. Toon, *Doctrine of the Trinity*.
86. 2 Cor 5:19.
87. Heb 9:16.

Becoming Theocentric

However, one must ask: Who is Christ? Unless the answer to that question is that Jesus of Nazareth is Emmanuel, very God in the flesh, the New Testament becomes a collection of confused assertions. Though the deity of Christ must be held by faith, faith can only be truly placed in Christ if the believer realizes who Christ is. This is not to state that one must have a perfect Christology in order to be saved ("no man knoweth who the Son is, but the Father"),[88] but he must be able to assert with the apostle Paul, "I know whom I have believed."[89] Nevertheless, to declare that Christ is God is also to open a world of inquiry into his nature. This is beneficial since the New Testament explains what it asserts.

Scripture is God's self-revelation to man. As part of Scripture the New Testament reveals the Godhead through the person of Christ. In order to understand who Christ is and what he did, believers must recognize his relation to the other two persons of the Trinity. While the majority of what believers know about the Son and the Spirit is found in the New Testament, this revelation instructs them on the ontology of all three of the persons of the Trinity, as far as their feeble capacity can understand. Trinitarian theology could not have been fully understood in the Old Testament without the light of the New Testament. Likewise, the New Testament cannot be properly understood and employed if trinitarian theology is ignored.[90] The life of faith lived in fellowship with the faithful demonstrates this well.

Although the church belongs to Christ as his purchased possession, apostolic writings regarding the church and its members display all three persons at work. Believers are taught to come to the Father by Christ, to pray to the Father in Christ Jesus' name, to pray in the Spirit, to worship God in spirit and in truth, which is understood as Christ himself since Jesus declared, "I am . . . the truth."[91] The content of the New Testament is "trinitarian theology" in that, as it is examined through eyes of faith, the Trinity is encountered

---

88. Luke 10:22.
89. 2 Tim 1:12.
90. Toon, *Our Triune God*, 78.
91. John 14:6.

everywhere, is more correctly understood, and is discovered to be the origin of all that the believer enjoys. "There is nothing that sounds new in all this—and yet to many of us it may be something quite new if we are clearly and consciously realising our distinct relationship to each Person of the Blessed Trinity."[92] The God to be worshiped is the Trinity and the Trinity is God.

Perhaps this interpretation of the New Testament as a whole is best crystallized in the general Epistle to the Hebrews. A gospel, an apology, a homily, a creed—the book of Hebrews begins with the relationship of the Son to the Father before the creation of time, space, and matter and also at the incarnation. The person of the Son is clearly contrasted to the angels and the saints, the honorable Moses in particular. While this teaching is represented as pertaining to mature Christian understanding, it is presented as the basis for salvation.[93]

The preexistence of Christ is demonstrated by comparing him to Melchizedek and contrasting him with the Levitical priesthood. The work of Christ necessitates this ontological difference. He came to offer the all-encompassing offering for the sins of the world. The means of this offering (the Spirit) and its receiver (the Father) turn attention to the broader scope of this tremendous event. The writer develops the believers' understanding of the Spirit by designating him eternal and by representing the gravity of refusing his invitation or of being insincere with him. Introduced at the opening of the book as the Father of the Son, the Father accepts the sacrifice of the Great High Priest and then becomes a Christian's own wise and loving parent. All of this is understood by faith because the nature and character of God are the fundamental elements in the believer's relationship to God.[94] The trinitarian framework developed throughout the book of Hebrews is the foundation of all that the New Testament teaches Christians to believe.

Once a believer begins to focus on who God is more than what he does, he will also be assisted in focusing on what God desires him

---

92. Hodgson, *Doctrine of the Trinity*, 179.
93. Heb 5:11—6:2.
94. Heb 10:13; 11:6.

Becoming Theocentric

to *be* instead of just what he should *do*. Hereby the image of God is reflected in man rather than man's image being projected onto God. This is the solution to Neo-nomianism. Increased knowledge of God includes increased reverence and proper fear of God. Realizing who is violated by sin and not merely his response to sin, as well as realizing who it is that is the Savior, instead of merely what he did to provide that salvation, offers a better basis for faith and worship. This knowledge leads to faith and reverence in worship because knowledge correlates to faith, thence to reverent humility, which reveals the duty to defend the faith as well as the attitude in which one ought to do it.[95]

The foremost result of all these spiritual changes is rest. The pastures of the Lord are always green, but he has to cause his sheep to lie down in them.[96] Faith naturally leads to a rest that will itself produce joy that transcends immediate circumstances. Faith raises a believer from himself and beyond his experiences as he focuses on God and rests in him. For this the believer must look beyond his own sufficiency and natural abilities and look to Christ alone.

Job's responses to his sufferings are an excellent example. At first he did not accuse God, but eventually he was baffled. His difficulty was not with the experience but with the mental roadblocks. He knew he was innocent. However when his friends accused him, he attempted to convince them and thereby reached his wits' end. His insistence on his innocence led his friends to the conclusion that Job thought God was unjust. When Job reacted to his friends' assumption, he succumbed to it. When God finally speaks, he offers no reason why these experiences happened to Job. Instead he demands of Job if he is able to work as God. God's work demonstrates that the Doer must have a different nature than mankind. This leads into the conclusion that *who* God *is* must be sufficient.

Faith, knowledge, rest, duty—without God, man would never be able to connect these four. Within faith in God, they can only be connected in that order. "And beside this, giving all diligence, add to your faith virtue; and to virtue knowledge; and to knowledge temperance;

---

95. E. Hopgood, personal communication to the author, July 20, 2013.
96. Ezek 34:15; Hos 2:18.

Earth Shadows on the Sky

and to temperance patience; and to patience godliness; and to godliness brotherly kindness; and to brotherly kindness charity."[97]

How could man ever hope to know God? Yet God specializes in hope.[98] All true hope must be in the person of God or, better said, in the persons of the Trinity. God desires our fellowship. Believers can fellowship with God as they comprehend who he is and understand him as a personal reality, real in himself and real in them.

On the other hand, a Christian must never imagine that he knows God in his entirety. The truth of apophatic theology lies in the immensity of God. As Gregory of Nazianzus expressed it, one may only see the glory of God, never his very person.[99] The one significant exception to this truth, nevertheless, does not deny it as a truth.

> God who at sundry times and in divers manners spake in time past unto the fathers by the prophets, hath in these last days spoken unto us by *his* Son, whom he hath appointed heir of all things, by whom also he made the worlds; who being the brightness of *his* glory, and the express image of his person, and upholding all things by the word of his power, when he had by himself purged our sins, sat down on the right hand of the Majesty on high.[100]

The fully developed doctrine of the Ontological Trinity is a profound subject. Studied diligently, it raises a man's consciousness from the common sense mode to the level of differentiated consciousness. This new intellectual level will greatly assist the believer in his study of the entire Scripture and system of Christian doctrine.

Together with all these benefits, and perhaps encompassing them, is the result that a knowledge of the developed doctrine of the Ontological Trinity will cause a believer's thinking to be more distinctly Christian. As he better understands the revealed, scriptural truth about the God he worships, he will be less susceptible to harmful influences, not only from pseudo-Christianity but also

---

97. 2 Pet 1:5–7.
98. Pss 22:9; 42:11; Rom 15:13.
99. Gregory of Nazianzus, *Five Theological Orations*, 22–23.
100. Heb 1:1–3.

Becoming Theocentric

from Judaism, Eastern religions, and popular culture. This protection will allow the believer to proclaim the pure gospel of Jesus Christ, both in word and deed. "This is the truth sent from above / The truth of God, the God of love."[101]

Dr. T. F. Torrance best summed up the challenge thus:

> By its very nature, therefore, faith in God is characterized by a kind of infinity; for while God as a 'whole' eludes our comprehension, what he does allow us to apprehend of himself is inseparable from what is as 'whole' so that it breaks through the narrow confines of our grasp. . . . Thus while God infinitely transcends the human mind he may nevertheless be known through a movement of faith in which it is opened toward the infinity and ineffability of God.[102]

This open-mindedness, while necessary to continue searching into the riches of the mystery of God, is at the same time a danger because it exposes a person to wrong ideas about God. If this gateway to infinity is properly guarded, however,

> Through faith we are brought into contact with God in such a way that we are enabled to know more than we can bring into explicit forms of thought or speech, and that in and through faith theology is engaged in a fathomless inquiry, for the truth which we seek to know is so deep that we can never probe it to its end, let alone reduce our knowledge of it to adequate formulation.[103]

For eternity, believers will explore the greatness of God in Christ.

As commanded, believers come to the Father in the name of his only Son, the Lord Jesus Christ, thanking and praising him for sending a Savior. Through the only begotten Son, the Father granted them grace to become dear children of God by the Spirit of adoption which is sent into their hearts, whereby they cry "Abba, Father."[104] The Spirit helps their infirmities since they do not know

---

101. Traditional English carol.
102. Torrance, *Trinitarian Faith*, 25–26.
103. Torrance, *Trinitarian Faith*, 25–26.
104. Rom 8:15; Toon, *Our Triune God*, 43–44.

what to pray for as they ought.[105] They also "have an advocate with the Father, Jesus Christ the righteous."[106] Though baptized in "the name of the Father, and of the Son, and of the Holy Ghost"[107] as Christ commanded, the wonderfulness of the Godhead, Three-in-One and One-in-Three, is beyond a believer's ability to comprehend. Nevertheless, the revelation of this truth in the word and the Holy Spirit's revealing the truth of the word to man is no slight cause of thanksgiving:[108] for the Father's great grace and compassion in sending Christ to reconcile us to himself; for Christ's great grace and humility who "made himself of no reputation, . . . was made in the likeness of men,"[109] and obediently suffered the death of the cross although he is equal with the Father; and for the great grace and condescension of the Holy Spirit who, though fully God, was willing to serve the Father and the Son and even man. Because of his great love and goodness, God preserves his elect by the grace and faith wherewith he saved them. He will not allow them to stray fatally from his truth in spite of their sin and error. God the Father, the Son, and the Holy Ghost has given himself to his own and taken them to himself in love by his grace. The whole Trinity loves and promises to come in and abide with believers if they but open the door.[110] In the Spirit, believers offer this worship, blessing, praise and glory to the Father through Jesus Christ the Lord.[111]

"O the depth of the riches both of the wisdom and knowledge of God! How unsearchable *are* his judgments and his ways past finding out! . . . For of him, and through him, and to him, *are* all things; to whom *be* glory for ever. Amen."[112]

---

105. Rom 8:26.
106. 1 John 2:1.
107. Matt 28:19.
108. Mascall, *Whatever Happened to the Human Mind?* 117–18.
109. Phil 2:7-8
110. Rev 3:20.
111. Toon, *Our Triune God*, 37.
112. Rom 11:33, 36.

Glossary

Apophatic theology—Negative theological statements, or asserting what God is not (i.e., not limited, not temporal, etc.).

Beatific Vision—The sight of God in glory as enjoyed by the souls in heaven; also the perfect communion with God such a sight implies (OED).

Cataphatic Theology—Positive theological statements, or asserting what God is.

Conciliar Period (c. AD 300–500)—The period from the Council of Nicaea until after the Council of Chalcedon during which time most of the ecumenical councils took place. The key orthodox leaders of this period were Alexander and Athanasius (successive bishops of Alexandria); Cyprian of Alexandria; Hilary of Portiers; and from Cappadocia, Basil the Great, Gregory of Nazianzus, and Gregory of Nyssa (known collectively as the Cappadocian Fathers). Prominent heretical and semi-heretical figures included Arius, Eusibius of Caesaria, and Nestorius.

Economic Trinity—The Holy Trinity considered from the perspective of God's dealings with man; God-as-God-is-toward-us.

Glossary

Economy of Grace—The providential and salvific work of God in and for his creation both before and during time. The economy of grace is particularly represented by the *missio Dei* (see *missio Dei*).

Enlightenment Era (c. AD 1600–1800)—A time characterized by emphasis on man's rights and abilities, especially to reason independently of church or state. This reasoning was predominantly empirically scientific and mathematic rather than philosophical. The key figures of the Enlightenment were Peter Ramus, John Locke, and René Descartes.

Federal Theology—God made a covenant of life with Adam as the federal head of the human race. Adam broke that covenant by his disobedience. God therefore made a covenant of grace with Christ for the salvation of fallen humanity (also known as the covenant of redemption).

Homoiousios (Gk. ὁμοιούσιος)—Of *like* substance (also spelled *homoeousios*).

Homoousios (Gk. ὁμοούσιος)—Of the *same* substance; consubstantial.

Ὁμοούσιος τῷ Πατρί (Homoousios tō Patri)—Of the same substance with the Father.

Hypostasis (Gk. ὑπόστασις)—In the fully formulated doctrine of the Trinity, *hypostasis* indicated a specific individual, a person, when applied to God or man.

Hypostatic Union—The joining of the two natures (full deity and complete, perfect humanity) in the Person of Christ Jesus.

Immanent Trinity—The Ontological Trinity.

Marcion (excommunicated AD 144)—Attributed the Old and New Testaments to two different gods, the Old Testament to an angry warrior god and the New Testament to the Father of Jesus Christ. For these reasons Marcion rejected the Old Testament and removed all positive references to it from the

Glossary

New Testament. He and his followers then made and actively circulated his revised edition of the Greek text.

"Mia ousia, tres hypostaseis" (Gk.)—"One essence, three Persons;" the Greek formula designating the unity and plurality of the Trinity.

Missio Dei (Ln.)—The sending into the world of the Son at the incarnation and the Spirit at Pentecost.

Modalism—The heretical teaching that the Father, the Son, and the Holy Spirit are three different modes of being or three different forms by which the single Person of God is expressed instead of three distinguishable Persons mutually indwelling one another and together one God. Mature Modalism is also termed Sabellianism.

Ontological Trinity—The Holy Trinity considered from the perspective of God's essence; the Godhead; God-as-God-is-in-himself. Also known as the Immanent Trinity.

Ontology—The essence of a person or thing; that which it is.

Ousia (Gk. οὐσία)—The nature or essence of a person or thing, especially that which it has in common with others.

Regula fidei (Ln.)—The Rule of Faith; the orthodox interpretation of the Scriptures encapsulated in the doctrines handed down in the church from the apostles. Also known as the "analogy of faith" or the "canon of faith."

Sabellianism—See Modalism.

Appendix

THE APOSTLES' CREED

I believe in God the Father Almighty, Maker of heaven and earth:
    And in Jesus Christ his only Son our Lord, Who was conceived by the holy Ghost, Born of the Virgin Mary, Suffered under Pontius Pilate, Was crucified, died, and buried, He descended into hell; The third day he rose again from the dead, He ascended into Heaven, And sitteth on the right hand of God the Father Almighty; From thence he shall come to judge the quick and the dead.
    I believe in the Holy Ghost; The holy Catholick Church; The Communion of Saints; The forgiveness of sins; The resurrection of the body, And the Life everlasting. Amen.[1]

THE NICENO-CONSTANTINOPOLITAN CREED

I believe in one God the Father Almighty, Maker of heaven and earth, And of all things visible and invisible:
    And in one Lord Jesus Christ, the only begotten son of God, Begotten of his Father before the worlds, God of God, Light of Light, Very God of very God, Begotten, not made, Being of one substance

---

[1]. All creed texts in this appendix are taken from *The Book of Common Prayer*, 1662.

Appendix

with the Father, By whom all things were made: Who for us men and for our salvation came down from heaven, And was incarnate by the holy Ghost of the Virgin Mary, And was made man, And was crucified also for us under Pontius Pilate. He suffered and was buried, And the third day he rose again according to the Scriptures, And ascended into heaven, And sitteth on the right hand of the Father. And he shall come again with glory to judge the quick and the dead: Whose kingdom shall have no end.

And I believe in the Holy Ghost, The Lord and giver of life, Who proceedeth from the Father and the Son, Who with the Father and the Son is to be worshipped and glorified, Who spake by the prophets. And I believe on Catholick and Apostolic Church. I acknowledge one Baptism for the remission of sins, And I look for the Resurrection of the dead, And the life of the world to come. Amen.

THE ATHANASIAN CREED—QUICUNQUE VULT

Whosoever will be saved: before all things it is necessary that he hold the Catholick Faith. Which Faith, except every one do keep whole and undefiled: without doubt he shall perish everlastingly. And the Catholick Faith is this: that we worship one God in Trinity, and Trinity in Unity; Neither confounding the persons: nor dividing the substance. For there is one person of the Father, another of the Son: and another of the Holy Ghost. But the Godhead of the Father, of the Son, and of the Holy Ghost, is all one: the Glory equal, the Majesty co-eternal. Such as the Father is, such is the Son: and such is the Holy Ghost. The Father uncreate, the Son uncreate: and the Holy Ghost uncreate. The Father incomprehensible, the Son incomprehensible: and the Holy Ghost incomprehensible. The Father eternal, the Son eternal: and the Holy Ghost eternal. And yet they are not three eternals: but one eternal. As also there are not three incomprehensibles, nor three uncreated: but one uncreated, and one incomprehensible. So likewise the Father is Almighty, the Son Almighty: and the Holy Ghost Almighty. And yet there are not three Almighties: but one Almighty. So the Father is God, the Son

Appendix

God: and the Holy Ghost is God. And yet there are not three Gods: but one God. So likewise the Father is Lord, the Son Lord: and the Holy Ghost Lord; And yet there are not three Lords: but one Lord. For like as we are compelled by the Christian verity: to acknowledge every person by himself to be God and Lord; So are we forbidden by the Catholick Religion: to say, There be three Gods, or three Lords. The Father is made of none: neither created, nor begotten. The Son is of the Father alone: not made, nor created, but begotten. The Holy Ghost is of the Father and the Son: neither made, nor created, nor begotten, but proceeding. So there is one Father, not three Fathers; one Son not three Sons: one Holy Ghost, not three Holy Ghosts. And in this Trinity none is afore, or after other: none is greater, or less than another; But the whole three persons are co-eternal together: and co-equal. So that in all things, as is aforesaid: the Unity in Trinity, and the Trinity in Unity is to be worshipped. He therefore, that will be saved: must think thus of the Trinity.

Furthermore, it is necessary to everlasting salvation: that he also believe rightly the Incarnation of our Lord Jesus Christ. For the right Faith is, that we believe and confess: that our Lord Jesus Christ, the Son of God, is God, and Man; God, of the substance of the Father, begotten before the worlds; and Man, of the substance of his Mother, born in the world: Perfect God and perfect Man: of a reasonable soul, and humane flesh subsisting; Equal to the Father, as touching his Godhead: and inferior to the Father, as touching his Manhood; Who, although he be God, and Man: yet he is not two, but one Christ; One; not by conversion of the Godhead into flesh: but by taking of the Manhood into God; One altogether; not by confusion of substance: but by unity of person. For as the reasonable soul and flesh is one man: so God and Man is one Christ. Who suffered for our salvation: descended into hell, rose again the third day from the dead. He ascended into heaven, he sitteth at the right hand of the Father, God Almighty: from whence he shall come to judge the quick and the dead. At whose coming all men shall rise again with their bodies: and shall give account for their own works. And they that have done good shall go into life everlasting: and

Appendix

they that have done evil into everlasting fire. This is the Catholick Faith: which except a man believe faithfully, he cannot be saved.

Glory be to the Father, and to the Son: and to the Holy Ghost; As it was in the beginning, is now, and ever shall be: world without end. Amen.

Bibliography

Ahlstrom, Sydney. *The Religious History of the American People*. New Haven: Yale University Press, 1972.

———. "Theology in America: A Historical Survey." In *The Shaping of the American Mind*, edited by James Ward Smith and A. Leland Jamison, 232–321. Princeton, NJ: Princeton University Press, 1961.

Alexander of Alexandria. "Epistles on the Arian Heresy and the Deposition of Arius." In *Fathers of the Third Century: Gregory Thaumaturgus, Dionysius the Great, Julius Africanus, Anatolius and Minor Writers, Methodius, Arnobius*, edited by Alexander Roberts and James Donaldson, 291–302. Ante-Nicene Fathers of the Christian Church 6. Grand Rapids: Eerdmans, 1978.

Anderson, David. "Introduction." In *On the Holy Spirit*, by Basil of Caesraea, translated by David Anderson, 7–13. Crestwood, New York: St. Vladimir's, 1980.

Anonymous. "A Summary of the Life, Writings, and Character, of the late Reverend and Learned John Gill, D. D." In *A Collection of Sermons and Tracts: in Two Volumes . . . To which are prefixed, memoirs of the life, writings, and character of the author*, by John Gill, 1:ix–xxxiv. London: Printed for G. Keith, 1773.

Athanasius of Alexandria. "Against the Arians." In *St. Athanasius: Select Works and Letters*, edited by Archibald Robertson, 303–447. A Select Library of the Nicene and Post-Nicene Fathers of the Christian Church, Second Series 4. New York: Christian Literature, 1892.

———. "Against the Arians I." In *Documents in Early Christian Thought*, edited by Maurice Wiles and Mark Santer, 26–31. Cambridge: Cambridge University Press, 2007.

———. "Against the Heathen (*Contra Gentes*)." In *St. Athanasius: Select Works and Letters*, edited by Archibald Robertson, 1–30. A Select Library of the

Bibliography

Nicene and Post-Nicene Fathers of the Christian Church, Second Series 4. New York: Christian Literature, 1892.

———. "Councils of Ariminum and Seleucia." In *St. Athanasius: Select Works and Letters*, edited by Archibald Robertson, 448–80. A Select Library of the Nicene and Post-Nicene Fathers of the Christian Church, Second Series 4. New York: Christian Literature, 1892.

———. "Defense of the Nicene Council (*De Decretis*)." In *St. Athanasius: Select Works and Letters*, edited by Archibald Robertson, 149–72. A Select Library of the Nicene and Post-Nicene Fathers of the Christian Church, Second Series 4. New York: Christian Literature, 1892.

———. "On the Incarnation (*De Incarnatione Verbi Dei*)." In *St. Athanasius: Select Works and Letters*, edited by Archibald Robertson, 31–67. A Select Library of the Nicene and Post-Nicene Fathers of the Christian Church, Second Series 4. New York: Christian Literature, 1892.

———. *St. Athanasius: Select Works and Letters*. Edited by Archibald Robertson. A Select Library of the Nicene and Post-Nicene Fathers of the Christian Church, Second Series 4. New York: Christian Literature, 1892.

"The Augsburg Confession, A.D. 1530." In *Creeds of Christendom: With a History and Critical Notes*, edited by Philip Schaff, revised by David S. Schaff, 3:3–73. 6th ed. 3 vols. Grand Rapids: Baker, 1998.

Augustine of Hippo. "Answer to Skeptics." In *Writings of Saint Augustine*, edited by Ludwig Schopp, 87–225. Fathers of the Church 1. New York: CIMA, 1948.

———. "Divine Providence and the Problem of Evil." In *Writings of Saint Augustine*, edited by Ludwig Schopp, 229–332. Fathers of the Church 1. New York: CIMA, 1948.

———. "Faith Seeking Understanding." In *Readings in the Philosophy of Religion*, edited by John A. Mourant, 255–62. New York: Crowell, 1954.

———. "The Happy Life." In *Writings of Saint Augustine*, edited by Ludwig Schopp, 29–84. Fathers of the Church 1. New York: CIMA, 1948.

———. "On Christian Doctrine, III." In *Documents in Early Christian Thought*, edited by Maurice Wiles and Mark Santer, 154–58. Cambridge: Cambridge University Press, 2007.

———. "On the Trinity IX." In *Documents in Early Christian Thought*, edited by Maurice Wiles and Mark Santer, 36–42. Cambridge: Cambridge University Press, 2007.

———. "Soliloquies." In *Writings of Saint Augustine*, edited by Ludwig Schopp, 335–426. Fathers of the Church 1. New York: CIMA, 1948.

———. *The Trinity* (*De Trinitate*). Translated by Steven McKenna. Fathers of the Church 45. New York, CIMA 1963.

———. *Writings of Saint Augustine*. Edited by Ludwig Schopp. Fathers of the Church, 1. New York: CIMA, 1948.

Basil of Caesarea. *On the Holy Spirit*. Translated by David Anderson. Crestwood, New York: St. Vladimir's, 1980.

Bibliography

"The Belgic Confession of Faith, 1561." In *Reformed Confessions of the Sixteenth Century*, edited by Arthur C. Cochrane, 185–219. 1966. Reprint, Louisville: Westminster/John Knox, 2003.

Benjamin, Jerry. *Simply Singular—Is Christ Prominent or Preeminent?* Little Nuggets Series. 2001. Reprint, Elm, PA: Executive Printing, 2015.

Bishop, William Samuel. *The Development of Trinitarian Doctrine in the Nicene and Athanasian Creeds: A Study in Theological Definition*. London: Longmans, Green, 1910.

Blunt, David. "Which Bible Version: Does It Really Matter?" London: Trinitarian Bible Society, 2007.

The Book of Common Prayer. Cambridge: Cambridge University Press, 1662.

Bunyan, John. *The Pilgrim's Progress*. 1895. Reprint, Edinburgh: Banner of Truth Trust, 2009.

Calhoun, Robert Lowry. *Scripture, Creed, Theology: Lectures on the History of Christian Doctrine in the First Centuries*. Edited by George A. Lindbeck. Eugene, OR: Cascade, 2011.

Calvin, John. *The Bondage and Liberation of the Will: A Defense of the Orthodox Doctrine of Human Choice against Pighius*. Translated by G. I. Davies. Edited by A. N. S. Lane. Texts & Studies in Reformation and Post-Reformation Thought. Grand Rapids: Baker, 1996.

———. *Commentaries on the Book of Joshua*. Translated by Henry Beveridge. Grand Rapids: Eerdmans, 1949.

———. *Commentary on a Harmony of the Evangelists, Matthew, Mark, and Luke*. Translated by William Pringle. Vols. 16–17 of Calvin's Commentaries. 22 vols. Reprint, Grand Rapids: Baker, 2009.

———. *Concerning the Eternal Predestination of God*. Translated by J. K. S. Reid. London: 1961.

———. *The Institutes of the Christian Religion*. Edited by John T. McNeill. Translated by Ford Lewis Battles. Louisville: Westminster/John Knox, 1960.

Cervantes, Miguel de. *Don Quixote*. Translated by John Rutherford. New York: Penguin, 2003.

Chaucer, Geoffrey. "Canterbury Tales." In *British Literature*, edited by Ronald A. Horton, 57–91. 2nd ed. Greenville, SC: Bob Jones University Press, 2003.

Chauncy, Charles. *The Benevolence of the Deity, Fairly and Impartially Considered*. Boston: 1784.

———. "Ministers Exhorted and Encouraged to take heed to themselves and their Doctrine." Boston: Printed by Rogers and Fowle, for S. Eliot in Cornhill, 1744.

———. *The Mystery Hid from Ages and Generations, or, The Salvation of All Men*. 1784. Reprint, New York: Arno, 1969.

———. "The New Creature Describ'd and Consider'd as the Sure Characteristick of Being in Christ: Together with Some Seasonable Advice to those who Are New Creatures." Boston: Printed by G. Rogers for J. Edwards and S. Eliot in Cornhill, 1741.

Bibliography

———. "The Only Compulsion Proper to Be Made Use of in the Affairs of Conscience and Religion." Boston: Printed by J. Draper for J. Edwards in Cornhill, 1739.

———. "The Opinion of One That Has Perused the Summer Morning's Conversation Concerning Original Sin, Wrote by the Rev. Mr. Peter Clark." Boston: Printed and sold by Green and Russell, 1758.

———. *Twelve Sermons on the Following Seasonable and Important Subjects, Justification Impossible by the Works of the Law. The Question Answered, "Wherefore then Serveth the Law?" The Nature of Faith, as Justifying, Largely Explained, and Remarked on. The Place, and Use, of Faith, in the Affair of Justification, Human Endeavours, in the Use of Means, The Way in which Faith Is Obtained . . . With Interspersed Notes, in Defence of the Truth, Especially in the Points Treated on, in the Above Discourses.* Boston: Printed by D. and J. Kneeland for Thomas Leverett, in Cornhill, 1765.

Chesterton, G. K. *Orthodoxy*. 1908. Reprint, San Francisco: Ignatius, 1995.

Clark, Peter. "The Scripture-Doctrine of Original Sin, Stated and Defended. In a Summer-Morning's Conversation, between a Minister and a Neighbor. Containing Remarks on a Late Anonymous Pamphlet intitled 'A Winter-Evening's Conversation, upon the Doctrine of Original Sin.'" Boston: Printed by Edes and Gill, 1758.

Clarke, Samuel. *A Discourse Concerning the Being and Attributes of God, the Obligations of Natural Religion, and the Truth and Certainty of the Christian Revelation*. London: Printed by W. Botham for J. and J. Knapton, 1732.

Clement of Rome. "The Letter of the Church of Rome to the Church of Corinth, Commonly Called Clement's First Letter." In *Early Christian Fathers*, edited by Cyril C. Richardson, 33–73. Louisville: Westminster John Knox, 1953.

Cochrane, Arthur C., ed. *Reformed Confessions of the Sixteenth Century*. 1966. Reprint, Louisville: Westminster/John Knox, 2003.

D'Aubingé, Jean Henri Merle. *History of the Reformation of the Sixteenth Century*. 1846. Reprint, Grand Rapids: Baker, 1976.

Descartes, René. "Certainty of Self and God (Meditations I–III)." In *Primary Readings in Philosophy for Understanding Theology*, edited by Diogenes Allen and Eric O. Springsted, 111–39. Louisville: Westminster/John Knox, 1992.

Dionysius of Alexandria. "On the Promises." In *Documents in Early Christian Thought*, edited by Maurice Wiles and Mark Santer, 145–51. Cambridge: Cambridge University Press, 2007.

Dionysius the Areopagite. "Our Knowledge of God." In *Readings in the Philosophy of Religion*, edited by John A. Mourant, 41–52. New York: Crowell, 1954.

Eusebius of Caesarea. "*Epistola Eusebii*." In *St. Athanasius: Select Works and Letters*, edited by Archibald Robertson, 73–76. A Select Library of the Nicene and Post-Nicene Fathers of the Christian Church, Second Series 4. New York: Christian Literature, 1892.

Bibliography

Faust, Clarence H., and Thomas H. Johnson. *Jonathan Edwards: Representative Selections, with Introduction, Bibliography, and Notes*. New York: Hill and Wang, 1962.

"The First Helvetic Confession of Faith of 1536." In *Reformed Confessions of the Sixteenth Century*, edited by Arthur C. Cochrane, 97–111. 1966. Reprint, Louisville: Westminster/John Knox, 2003.

"The Formula of Concord, A.D. 1576." In *Creeds of Christendom: With a History and Critical Notes*, edited by Philip Schaff, revised by David S. Schaff, 3:93–180. 6th ed. 3 vols. Grand Rapids: Baker, 1998.

Fortman, Edmund J. *The Triune God: A Historical Study of the Doctrine of the Trinity*. Philadelphia: Westminster, 1972.

Foxgrover, David. "Self-Examination in John Calvin and William Ames." In *Later Calvinism: International Perspectives*, edited by Fred Graham, 451–69. Sixteenth Century Essays and Studies 22. Kirksville, MO: Sixteenth Century Journal, 1994.

Franklin, Benjamin. "The Autobiography." In *American Literature*, edited by Raymond A. St. John, 96–104. 2nd ed. Greenville, SC: Bob Jones University Press, 2010.

"The French Confession of Faith, 1559." In *Reformed Confessions of the Sixteenth Century*, edited by Arthur C. Cochrane, 137–58. 1966. Reprint, Louisville: Westminster/John Knox, 2003.

Fretheim, Terence E. *Exodus*. Interpretation: A Bible Commentary for Teaching and Preaching. Louisville: John Knox, 1991.

Gammie, John G. "A Journey through Danielic Spaces: The Book of Daniel in the Theology and Piety of the Christian Community." In *Interpreting the Prophets*, edited by James Luther Mays and Paul J. Achtemeier, 261–72. Philadelphia: Fortress, 1987.

Gill, John. *The Cause of God and Truth*. 4th ed. London: Printed for G. Keith, 1775.

———. *A Collection of Sermons and Tracts: In Two Volumes . . . To Which Are Prefixed, Memoirs of the Life, Writings, and Character of the Author*. London: Printed for G. Keith, 1773.

———. *Complete Body of Doctrinal and Practical Divinity: Or, A System of Evangelical Truths Deduced from the Sacred Scriptures*. 3 vols. London: Printed for Winterbotham, 1796.

———. "A Dissertation Concerning the Eternal Sonship of Christ." In *A Collection of Sermons and Tracts: In Two Volumes . . . To which are prefixed, memoirs of the life, writings, and character of the author*, by John Gill, 2:534–64. London: Printed for G. Keith, 1773.

———. *The Doctrine of Justification by the Righteousness of Christ, Stated and Maintained, Being the Substance of Several Sermons*. 3rd. ed. London: Printed by H. Woodfall, 1750.

———. *The Doctrine of the Trinity, Stated and Vindicated. Being the Substance of Several Discourses on that Important Subject; reduc'd into the form of a treatise*. London: Printed and sold by Aaron Ward and H. Whitridge, 1731.

Bibliography

———. *The Doctrines of God's Everlasting Love to His Elect, and Their Eternal Union With Christ: together with some other truths, stated and defended. In a letter to Mr. (alias Dr.) Abraham Taylor*. London: Printed and sold by A. Ward and H. Whitridge, 1732.

Graham, Fred, ed. *Later Calvinism: International Perspectives*. Sixteenth Century Essays and Studies 22. Kirksville, MO: Sixteenth Century Journal, 1994.

Gregory of Nazianzus. *Faith Gives Fullness to Reasoning: The Five Theological Orations*. Translated by Frederick W. Norris. Leiden: Brill, 1900.

———. *The Five Theological Orations of Gregory of Nazianzus*. Edited by Arthur James Mason. Cambridge: Cambridge University Press, 1899.

Griffin, Edward M. *Old Brick, Charles Chauncy of Boston, 1705-1787*. Minneapolis: University of Minnesota Press, 1980.

Guelzo, Allen C. "Puritanism, American." In *Encyclopedia of the Reformed Faith*, 308-10.

Haakonssen, Knud, ed. *Enlightenment and Religion: Rational Dissent in Eighteenth-Century Britain*. Cambridge: Cambridge University Press, 1996

Hägglund, Bengt. *History of Theology*. Translated by Gene J. Lund. St. Louis: Concordia, 1968.

Hahn, Scott W. *Kinship by Covenant: A Canonical Approach to the Fulfillment of God's Saving Promises*. New Haven: Yale University Press, 2009.

Hannah, John D. *Charts of Reformation and Enlightenment Church History*. Grand Rapids: Zondervan, 2004.

Hanson, R. P. C. *The Search for the Christian Doctrine of God: The Arian Controversy, 318-381*. Edinburgh: T. & T. Clark, 1988.

Haykin, Michael A. G., ed. *The British Particular Baptists, 1638-1910*. 3 vols. Springfield, MS: Particular Baptist, 1998.

"The Heidelberg Catechism, 1536." In *Reformed Confessions of the Sixteenth Century*, edited by Arthur C. Cochrane, 305-31. 1966. Reprint, Louisville: Westminster/John Knox, 2003.

Hill, William J. *The Three-Personed God: The Trinity as a Mystery of Salvation*. Washington, DC: The Catholic University Press, 1982.

Hodgson, Leonard. *The Doctrine of the Trinity: Croall Lectures, 1942-1943*. New York: Scribner's Sons, 1944.

Horton, Ronald A., ed. *British Literature*. 2nd ed. Greenville, SC: Bob Jones University Press, 2011.

Irenaeus of Lyons. "Against the Heresies III." In *Documents in Early Christian Thought*, edited by Maurice Wiles and Mark Santer, 128-32. Cambridge: Cambridge University Press, 2007.

James, Sydney V., ed. *The New England Puritans*. New York: Harper & Row, 1968.

Justin Martyr. "The First Apology of Justin, the Martyr." In *Early Christian Fathers*, edited by Cyril C. Richardson, 242-89. Louisville: Westminster John Knox, 1953.

Kelly, J. N. D. *Early Christian Doctrines*. 5th ed. London: Continuum International, 2000.

Bibliography

Klauber, Martin I. "Reformed Orthodoxy in Transition: Bénédict Pictet (1655–1724) and Enlightened Orthodoxy in Post-Reformation Geneva." In *Later Calvinism: International Perspectives*, edited by Fred Graham, 93–113. Sixteenth Century Essays and Studies 22. Kirksville, MO: Sixteenth Century Journal, 1994.

Kuklick, Bruce. *Churchmen and Philosophers: From Jonathan Edwards to John Dewey*. New Haven: Yale University Press, 1985.

Latourette, Kenneth Scott. *A History of Christianity*. Vol. 1: *Beginnings to A.D. 1500*. 1975. 2 vols. Reprint, HarperSanFrancisco, 1999.

Lim, Paul C. H. *Mystery Unveiled: The Crisis of the Trinity in Early Modern England*. Oxford Studies in Historical Theology. Oxford: Oxford University Press, 2012.

Lindblad, Don. "Jesus Weeps." Sermon, Trinity Reformed Baptist Church, Kirkland, WA, October 22, 2017.

Linden, Glenn. "Charles Chauncy." MA thesis, University of Washington, 1957.

Lippy, Charles H. *Seasonable Revolutionary: The Mind of Charles Chauncy*. Chicago: Nelson-Hall, 1981.

Lonergan, Bernard. *The Way to Nicea: The Dialectical Development of Trinitarian Theology*. London: Darton, Longman & Todd, 1976.

Maclear, James Fulton. "'The Heart of New England Rent': The Mystical Element in Early Puritan History." In *The New England Puritans*, edited by Sydney V. James, 43–65. New York: Harper & Row, 1968.

Madueme, Hans. "Adam and Evolution: Insights from *Sola Scriptura*." Lecture, annual meeting of the Alliance of Christian Musicians, Tacoma, WA, November 4, 2017.

Maritain, Jacques. *Science and Wisdom*. Translated by Bernard Wall. 1940. Reprint, New York: Scribner's Sons, 1954.

———. *True Humanism*. New York: Scribner's Sons, 1938.

Mascall, E. L. *Christ, the Christian, and the Church: A Study of the Incarnation and Its Consequences*. London: Longmans, Greene, 1946.

———. "Is Theological Discourse Possible?" In *Readings in the Philosophy of Religion*, edited by John A. Mourant, 262–70. New York: Crowell, 1954.

———. *Whatever Happened to the Human Mind?* London: SPCK, 1980.

May, Henry. *The Enlightenment in America*. New York: Oxford University Press, 1976.

Mays, James Luther, and Paul J. Achtemeier, eds. *Interpreting the Prophets*. Philadelphia: Fortress, 1987.

McBeth, H. Leon, ed. *A Sourcebook for Baptist Heritage*. Nashville: Broadman, 1990.

McKim, Donald K., ed. *Encyclopedia of the Reformed Faith*. Edinburgh: St. Andrew's, 1992.

———. "Ramus, Peter (1515–1572)." In *Encyclopedia of the Reformed Faith*, 314.

Miller, Perry. "The Marrow of Puritan Divinity." In *The New England Puritans*, edited by Sydney V. James, 12–42. New York: Harper & Row, 1968.

Bibliography

Mourant, John A., ed. *Readings in the Philosophy of Religion.* New York: Crowell, 1954.

Nichols, James Hastings. *History of Christianity, 1650-1950: Secularization of the West.* New York: Ronald, 1956.

Norris, Richard A., Jr. "I Believe in God, the Father Almighty *Credo in deum patrem omnipotentem.*" In *Exploring and Proclaiming the Apostles' Creed,* edited by Roger Van Harn, 20-32. Grand Rapids: Eerdmans, 2004.

Oliver, Robert W. "John Gill (1697-1771)." In *The British Particular Baptists, 1638-1910,* edited by Michael A. G. Haykin, 1:144-65. 3 vols. Springfield, MS: Particular Baptist, 1998.

Olson, Roger E., ed. *The Westminster Handbook to Evangelical Theology.* Louisville: Westminster John Knox, 2004.

Pelikan, Jaroslav. *Bach among the Theologians.* Philadelphia: Fortress, 1986.

Perkins, William. "A Chart of Salvation and Damnation." In *Puritanism in Tudor England,* edited by H. C. Porter, 295-300. Columbia: University of South Carolina Press, 1971.

———. "Letter No. 9, Epistle to the Reader." In *Puritanism in Tudor England,* edited by H. C. Porter, 291-93. Columbia: University of South Carolina Press, 1971.

Pohle, Joseph. *The Divine Trinity: A Dogmatic Treatise.* Translated by Arthur Preuss. 6th ed. St. Louis: Herder, 1930.

Porter, H. C., ed. *Puritanism in Tudor England.* Columbia, SC: University of South Carolina Press, 1971.

Prestige, G. L. *Fathers and Heretics: Six Studies in Dogmatic Faith.* New York: Macmillan, 1940.

Quasten, Johannes. *Patrology.* 3 vols. Westminster, MD: Newman, 1962.

Richardson, Cyril, ed. *Early Christian Fathers.* Louisville: Westminster John Knox, 1953.

Sant, Henry. "John Gill: The Man and His Ministry." Southampton, UK: Huntingtonian, n.d.

Schaff, Philip, ed. *Creeds of Christendom: With a History and Critical Notes.* 6th ed. Revised by David S. Schaff. 3 vols. Grand Rapids: Baker, 1998.

"The Second Helvetic Confession, 1566." In *Reformed Confessions of the Sixteenth Century,* edited by Arthur C. Cochrane, 220-301. 1966. Reprint, Louisville: Westminster/John Knox, 2003.

Shadley, Karl E., Jr. "Leading Trinitarian Incarnational Worship: The Essential Work of the Pastorate." DMin diss., Fuller Theological Seminary, 1996.

The Shorter Oxford English Dictionary. 6th ed. Oxford: Oxford University Press, 2007.

Spitz, Lewis W. *The Renaissance and Reformation Movements.* Vol. 2, *The Reformation.* Revised ed. 2 vols. St. Louis: Concordia, 1987.

St. John, Raymond A., ed. *American Literature for Christian Schools.* 2nd ed. Greenville, SC: Bob Jones University Press, 2010.

Stout, Harry S. *The New England Soul: Preaching and Religious Culture in Colonial New England.* New York: Oxford University Press, 1986.

Bibliography

Studer, Basil. *Trinity and Incarnation*. Translated by Andrew Louth. Collegeville, MN: Liturgical, 1993.

Theodore of Mopsuestia. "Commentary on Galatians 4:24." In *Documents in Early Christian Thought*, edited by Maurice Wiles and Mark Santer, 151–54. Cambridge: Cambridge University Press, 2007.

Timiadis, Emilianos. *The Nicene Creed: Our Common Faith*. Philadelphia: Fortress, 1983.

Toon, Peter. *The Development of Doctrine in the Church*. Grand Rapids: Eerdmans, 1979.

———. *Doctrine of the Trinity*. Grand Rapids: Institute of Theological Studies, 2009. 2 CDs.

———. *The Emergence of Hyper-Calvinism in English Nonconformity, 1689–1765*. 1967. Reprint, Eugene, OR: Wipf & Stock, 2011.

———. *Our Triune God: A Biblical Portrayal of the Trinity*. Vancouver: Regent College, 2002.

Torrance, T. F. *The Christian Doctrine of God, One Being, Three Persons*. Edinburgh: T. & T. Clark, 1996.

———. *The Trinitarian Faith: The Evangelical Theology of the Ancient Church*. Edinburgh: T. & T. Clark, 1988.

Tyndale, William. "An Answer unto Sir Thomas More's Dialogue." In *British Literature*, edited by Ronald A. Horton, 136–38. 2nd ed. Greenville, SC: Bob Jones University Press, 2003.

Van Harn, Roger, ed. *Exploring and Proclaiming the Apostles' Creed*. Grand Rapids: Eerdmans, 2004.

Wainwright, Geoffrey. "Foreword." In *Exploring and Proclaiming the Apostles' Creed*, edited by Roger Van Harn, ix–xi. Grand Rapids: Eerdmans, 2004.

Walker, Williston. *The Creeds and Platforms of Congregationalism*. New York: Scribner's Sons, 1893.

———. *Ten New England Leaders*. New York: Silver, Burnett, 1901.

Wallace, Dewey D., Jr. "Puritanism, English." In *Encyclopedia of the Reformed Faith*, 310–11.

Webb, R. K. "Emergence of Rational Dissent." In *Enlightenment and Religion: Rational Dissent in Eighteenth-Century Britain*, edited by Knud Haakonssen, 12–41. Cambridge: Cambridge University Press, 1996.

Wiles, Maurice. *The Making of Christian Doctrine: A Study in the Principles of Early Doctrinal Development*. Cambridge: Cambridge University Press, 1967.

Wiles, Maurice, and Mark Santer, eds. *Documents in Early Christian Thought*. Cambridge: Cambridge University Press, 2007.

General Index

Apologists, 2
Apostle, 6–7, 9, 14, 16–17, 21, 27, 35–37, 45, 114–15, 123
Argument(s), 2, 5–6, 16, 18, 74, 98
Arianism, 14, 41–45, 50, 66, 77
    Arius, 41–42, 44, 48, 66, 114, 121
    Arians, 43–44, 49–51, 110
Athanasian Creed. *See* Creed.
Athanasius, 47, 51–52, 54, 66, 110, 121
Augustine, 16–17, 19, 99

Basil the Great (of Caesarea), 42, 51, 121

Calvin, John, 5, 55–58, 62–65, 67, 86, 97–98
Calvinism, 84, 98 (*See also* Reformed.)
Calvinist, 64, 72, 79
Chauncy, Charles, xii–xiii, 65, 69–89, 92–95, 97, 103, 105–6, 108, 110, 114
Christian, Christianity, 18, 21–22, 31, 35, 39–41, 43–44, 53, 55, 83, 86, 88, 93, 98, 101, 103, 106, 112, 116, 118, 127

Church, xiii, 2–4, 6, 13–18, 20–21, 29, 32, 34–36, 39–41, 43, 45–46, 48, 52–57, 59, 65, 70, 81, 83–86, 89–90, 92, 100, 102, 108, 110, 112, 114–15, 122–23, 125–26
Clarke, Samuel, 4, 66
Conciliar, conciliar period. *See* Council.
Confession, 3, 17–18, 35, 37–39, 49, 68, 92, 110
    Augsburg Confession, A.D. 1530, 17
    Belgic Confession of Faith, 1561, 17
    French Confession of Faith, 1559, 16
    First Confession of Basel, 1534, 17
    First Helvetic Confession of 1536, 17
    Second Helvetic Confession, 1566, 16
Council, xiii, 2–4, 6, 14, 44–46, 48, 50, 52–54, 56–57, 66, 121
    of Chalcedon, 53, 121
    of Constantinople, 50, 52–53

General Index

Council (continued)
  of Nicaea (Nicea), 3, 45, 48, 50, 52–53, 121
Covenant, 37, 63, 66–68, 77, 80–81, 84, 92–93, 95, 109, 111, 114, 122
  of grace/redemption, 66–67, 77, 92–93, 95, 122
Creation. See Nature.
Creed, xiii, 11–12, 17–18, 21, 35–36, 45–50, 52–57, 90, 103, 116, 125–28
  Apostles' Creed, 18, 36, 125
  Athanasian Creed, 18, 54, 100, 126
  Nicene (Niceno-Constantinopolitan) Creed, 18, 27, 36, 45, 47–48, 50, 52–53, 125

Doctrine, xii, 4, 10, 11–16, 20–21, 36, 39, 41, 44–45, 48, 53–55, 57–58, 60–61, 64–68, 72, 81, 84–85, 88, 90, 98, 101–2, 104, 108, 110, 114, 118
  false doctrine, 14–15

Economic Trinity, 30, 32–33, 36–37, 39, 55, 65–66, 104, 109–10, 114, 121
Economy of grace/redemption. See Grace.
Election, predestination, xii, 17, 62–64, 71–72, 78–79, 81, 91, 93–94, 110–11, 113, 120
Enlightenment, 3–6, 15, 19, 55–57, 60, 62, 69, 74, 79–80, 84, 86, 88–89, 91, 99, 105, 112, 114, 122
Essence. See Ontology.
Evidence, empirical, 5, 22, 97
  of grace. See Grace.

Experience, 2, 4–6, 32, 40, 71, 74, 81, 83, 85, 103–104, 106, 117
Exposition, 3, 8–9, 17, 31, 36, 39–40, 48

Father, the, 4, 27–38, 40, 42–43, 47–53, 62, 66–67, 77–78, 92–95, 100, 105, 108–110, 115–16, 119–20, 122–23, 125–28
Fathers, ancient, 2–3, 15–18, 39–40, 44–47, 49, 55, 57, 86, 90, 114, 121

Gill, John, xii–xiii, 69, 88–98, 105, 107–8, 110, 114
Grace, 13, 18, 30, 32–33, 36–37, 39, 49, 61, 63–64, 66–67, 71, 76–78, 81–82, 92, 96, 103, 110, 112, 119–20, 122
  economy of grace/redemption, 30, 32–33, 36, 39, 49, 53, 67, 96, 112, 122
  evidences of grace, 71, 82–83, 112
  means of grace, 71, 77, 81–82, 109
Gregory of Nazianzus, 51, 118, 121
Gregory of Nyssa, 51, 121

Heresy, 2–3, 9, 13–14, 16, 18, 40, 44, 50, 54–56, 70, 90–91, 95, 105, 121, 123
Heretic, heretical. See Heresy.
Holy Ghost, the (Holy Spirit), 4–10, 14, 20, 22, 29–39, 42–43, 49–50, 52, 58, 62–63, 66–67, 71, 77–78, 81, 83, 95, 97, 100, 105, 108–9, 112–13, 115–16, 119–20, 123, 125–128
Homoiousios (Gk. ὁμοιούσιος), 50–51, 122

General Index

Homoousios (Gk.ὁμοούσιος), 47–48, 51–52, 122
Hyper-Calvinism, hyper-Calvinist, xii, 64–65, 67, 72, 77, 93, 98
Hypostasis (Gk.ὑπόστασις), 47, 51–52, 55, 122–23

Intellect, intellectual, 6, 11, 19–21, 46, 54, 83, 96, 100, 118 (*See also* Reason.)

Knowledge, xiii, 5–7, 11, 15, 19–20, 36, 39, 46, 59–60, 74, 90, 117–20

Luther, Martin, 16, 56, 58

Misconceptions, xi–xii, 27, 63, 65–67, 94, 100, 106
Misunderstanding. *See* Misconceptions.
Mystery, 3, 5, 33, 48–49, 55, 83, 114, 119

Natural, 7–8, 19, 24, 26, 31, 58, 60, 79, 85, 87, 102, 107, 117
Natural theology, natural religion. *See* Theology.
Nature, creation, xi, 2, 4–6, 19, 24, 28, 31, 33, 36, 42–44, 49, 60, 62, 68, 73–75, 79–80, 84–86, 95, 97, 99, 100, 105–7, 111–13, 116, 122
Nature, human, 4, 8, 10, 60, 73, 75, 79, 98, 101, 105, 117, 122
Nature of God. *See* Ontology.
New Testament, 7, 9, 28–29, 32, 34, 37, 49, 76, 114–16, 122–23

Old Testament, 9, 28, 115, 122
Ontology, essence, xi–xii, 1, 3, 5, 24–33, 37–40, 42–43, 48–55, 59, 63–65, 67, 73–75, 79–80, 83–84, 86, 92–96, 100, 104–8, 110–17, 122–23
Orthodox, orthodoxy, xiii, 2–3, 5–6, 14, 17–18, 30, 35, 44–45, 48–51, 53, 55, 59, 63, 66, 70, 86, 90–94, 98, 107, 121, 123

Paul, Apostle, 6–7, 21, 35, 114–15
Philosophy, philosophical, xi–xiii, 3–5, 10, 12, 16, 18–19, 21–22, 36, 40–44, 46–47, 49, 51, 53, 56, 59–60, 68–69, 72, 114, 122
Predestination. *See* Election.
Protestant, xiii, 5–6, 16–17, 56–58, 86, 109
Puritan, xii–xiii, 56–57, 59–62, 64, 66–72, 75–76, 78, 80–87, 90–95, 97, 107

Ramus, Peter, 59, 122
Rationalism, rationalists, xii, 6, 16, 44, 56–57, 59–62, 66, 69–72, 83, 85–86, 96–98, 101, 105–6
Reason, reasoning, xi–xii, 4–6, 10, 13, 18–21, 26, 41, 44, 49, 56–57, 59–60, 62, 64, 68, 72–74, 79–80, 82–88, 90, 96–104, 107, 117, 122
Reasonable, 4, 12, 84, 90, 98, 127
Unreasonable, irrational, 5, 15–16, 83, 89, 101
Reformation, 16, 56–58, 91, 93
Post-Reformation, 15, 55–56, 58, 114
Reformed, xii, 17, 55, 57, 59, 64–65, 67–68, 80–81, 90, 95, 107
Reformers, xiii, 16–18, 56–58, 64, 86

General Index

Regula fidei. See Rule of Faith.
Rest, 8, 60, 64, 83, 101, 112, 117
Revelation, xi, 5, 8, 10, 19, 22, 24–31, 43, 46–48, 51–53, 58–59, 68, 85–86, 97, 100, 103, 105, 114–15, 120
Rule of Faith, *Regula fidei*, 13–14, 17, 35, 45, 47, 57, 86, 102, 123

Salvation. See Soteriology.
Sanctification, 18, 62, 64, 71, 80, 93
Scripture, xii, 1–22, 25, 28–31, 33–34, 36–37, 39–40, 42–46, 48–49, 53, 55–60, 62–63, 67, 70, 73–74, 84–86, 90, 94, 97–104, 107–8, 115, 118
Son, the, 4, 28–38, 42, 47–52, 63, 66, 77, 92, 95, 100, 105, 110, 114–16, 120, 123, 126–28
Soteriology, xi, 1, 27, 31–32, 34, 37, 39, 43–44, 49, 58–67, 72, 74–75, 77, 79–85, 92–93, 95, 107–10, 113, 116–17, 122, 126–27

Sovereignty, xi–xiii, 24, 28, 33, 38, 63–65, 77–79, 92–95, 99–100, 106, 109, 111–13

Theology, xi, xiii–xiv, 1, 4–5, 12, 16, 18–22, 35, 44, 51–52, 56–58, 60, 63–64, 66–69, 71–73, 80, 83–87, 91–96, 100–2, 108, 114–15, 118–19, 121–22
Natural theology, natural religion, 4, 26, 63, 71–73, 85–86, 102, 106

Understanding, 6–8, 10–12, 20, 24, 27–29, 31, 46–48, 55, 58–59, 65, 67, 74, 99, 107, 112–14, 116
Unorthodox, 87, 108

Works, 60, 62, 75–76, 82–83, 127
of God, 8, 18, 25, 27, 29, 33, 37, 55, 60, 64, 67, 75, 86, 92, 96–97, 100, 104, 107–8, 112, 116, 122
Writings, written works, 13–14, 16, 39, 56, 60, 90–92, 96

Author Index

Ahlstrom, Sydney, 75, 81–83
Alexander of Alexandria, 42–43
Anderson, David, 50
Anonymous, 88–90, 92
Athanasius of Alexandria, 2–3, 15,
    24–25, 28, 31, 43, 50–51,
    108–10
Augustine of Hippo, 8, 10, 14, 17,
    19, 24, 29, 37, 44, 99, 104,
    107, 113

Basil the Great (of Caesarea), 27–
    29, 32–33, 39, 42–43, 49
Benjamin, Jerry, 6, 61, 106, 111
Bishop, William Samuel, xiv,
    45–46, 55
Blunt, David, 14, 108
Bunyan, John, 22, 61

Calhoun, Robert Lowry, 40, 43–44,
    50–51, 53
Calvin, John (Jean), 5, 7, 9, 16–17,
    19–20, 24, 55, 58, 62, 64,
    67, 86, 97, 100, 106, 113
Cervantes, Miguel de, 103
Chaucer, Geoffrey, 93
Chauncy, Charles, 73–85, 87, 105

Chesterton, G. K., 15
Clark, Peter, 72
Clarke, Samuel, 4
Cochrane, Arthur C., 17

D'Aubigné, Jean Henri Merle, 91
Descartes, René, 60
Dionysius of Alexandria, 2
Dionysius the Areopagite, 3,
    24–25, 33

Eusebius of Caesarea, 3

Faust, Clarence H., and Thomas H.
    Johnson, 103
Fortman, Edmund J., 40, 42–44,
    47–48, 51–52, 54–55.
Foxgrover, David, 59, 61
Fretheim, Terence E., 26

Gammie, John G., 1
Gill, John, 79, 90, 92–98
Gregory of Nazianzus, 7, 39, 42,
    47, 118
Griffin, Edward M., 70, 76, 80
Guelzo, Allen C., 69

Author Index

Hägglund, Bengt, 40, 50
Hahn, Scott W., 29, 113
Hannah, John D., 59, 71
Hanson, R. P. C., 43
Hill, William J., 30, 35–36
Hodgson, Leonard, 103, 116

Irenaeus of Lyons, 14

James, Sydney V., 70
Justin Martyr, 2

Kelly, J. N. D., 2–3, 14–15, 45, 66, 77
Klauber, Martin I., 58
Kuklick, Bruce, 5

Latourette, Kenneth Scott, 3, 9
Lim, Paul C. H., 61, 65–66, 89
Lindblad, Don, 111
Linden, Glenn, 71, 86–87
Lippy, Charles H., 70–72, 77–78, 81–84, 103, 108
Longergan, Bernard, 11–13

Maclear, James Fulton, 71–72
Madueme, Hans, 86
Maritain, Jacques, 19, 22
Mascall, E. L., xi, 7–8, 10–11, 13, 19, 21, 25, 28–29, 52, 78, 102, 109–10, 120
May, Henry, 5, 15–16, 27, 58, 60, 63, 96
McBeth, H. Leon, 91
McKim, Donald K., 59
Miller, Perry, 63, 68, 71, 74, 76, 78, 81, 83–84, 97

Nichols, James Hastings, 56–57, 59–60, 74, 77, 79, 83–84, 91

Norris, Richard A., Jr., 35

Oliver, Robert W., xii, 89–90, 105
Olson, Roger E., 108

Pelikan, Jaroslav, 5, 16
Perkins, William, 60, 63, 66
Pohle, Joseph, 38
Prestige, G. L., 12, 20

Quasten, Johannes, 36–37, 40–42

Sant, Henry, 90
Schaff, Philip, 13, 21
Shadley, Karl E., Jr., 109
Spitz, Lewis W., 16, 58
St. John, Raymond A., 107
Stout, Harry S., 71, 81
Studer, Basil, 24, 30–33, 35–41, 47–52, 53, 55

Theodore of Mopsuestia, 9
Timiadis, Emilianos, 100, 105, 107
Toon, Peter, 4–6, 12–13, 18, 30–31, 33, 37, 45, 49, 51–52, 54–56, 58–59, 61–66, 76, 85, 89, 93–95, 105, 110–11, 114–15, 119–20
Torrance, T. F., 27, 31–34, 36, 41–42, 45–55, 119
Tyndale, William, 8–9, 58

Wainwright, Geoffrey, 46
Walker, Williston, 69–70, 72–73, 77–78, 82, 87
Wallace, Dewey D., Jr., 57, 60–61
Webb, R. K., 4–6, 57, 59, 61, 66
Wiles, Maurice, 4, 16, 21, 41, 44, 104

www.ingramcontent.com/pod-product-compliance
Lightning Source LLC
Chambersburg PA
CBHW072142160426
43197CB00012B/2214